John Disturnell

Tourist's Guide to the Mississippi River

Giving all the railroad and steamboat routes diverging from Chicago, Milwaukee, and Dubuque, toward St. Paul, and the falls of St. Anthony

John Disturnell

Tourist's Guide to the Mississippi River
Giving all the railroad and steamboat routes diverging from Chicago, Milwaukee, and Dubuque, toward St. Paul, and the falls of St. Anthony

ISBN/EAN: 9783337411138

Printed in Europe, USA, Canada, Australia, Japan

Cover: Foto ©Lupo / pixelio.de

More available books at **www.hansebooks.com**

TOURIST'S GUIDE

TO THE

UPPER MISSISSIPPI RIVER:

GIVING ALL THE

RAILROAD AND STEAMBOAT ROUTES

DIVERGING FROM

CHICAGO, MILWAUKEE, AND DUBUQUE, TOWARD ST. PAUL, AND THE FALLS OF ST. ANTHONY;

ALSO,

RAILROAD AND STEAMBOAT ROUTES

FROM CHICAGO AND MILWAUKEE TO LAKE SUPERIOR;

TOGETHER WITH AN ACCOUNT OF

CITIES AND VILLAGES, AND OBJECTS OF INTEREST, ON THE ROUTE AND IN THE

UPPER VALLEY OF THE MISSISSIPPI.

With Tables of Distances, etc., and Map and Illustrations.

COMPILED BY J. DISTURNELL.

NEW YORK:
PUBLISHED BY THE AMERICAN NEWS COMPANY,
121 NASSAU STREET.
1866.

TO THE PUBLIC.

DURING the autumn of 1854, the Compiler of the "GUIDE TO THE UPPER MISSISSIPPI RIVER" sailed from Chicago, passing through Lake Michigan, and visited the far-famed Island of Mackinac and the Saut Ste. Marie, experiencing for the most part of the time, a continuation of delightful weather. This trip was convincing proof that the climate and health-restoring properties of this northern region, surrounded by pure bodies of water, was truly astonishing. In 1856, Lake Superior was visited and explored along its south shore, affording further evidence of the purity and healthiness of this whole Lake Region, extending for hundreds of miles westward, embracing the sources of the Upper Mississippi.

In 1857 appeared the "TRIP THROUGH THE GREAT LAKES AND THE ST. LAWRENCE RIVER," giving a detailed account of the then lines of travel—the beauties of the River and Lake scenery, and the healthy influence of the climate surrounding the Upper Lakes, or Inland Seas of America. Other visits since have been further convincing proofs, together with the testimony of many living witnesses, that this extensive country, for hundreds or thousands of miles north-westward, possesses the same recuperative and healthy influence on the human frame.

With these convictions, the writer visited the Upper Mississippi in 1865, proceeding as far north as St. Paul, and the Falls of St. Anthony, now the favorite resort of thousands of invalids, seeking health and pleasure. By going farther north-west, the same beneficial results are experienced, showing conclusively that consumptive patients, and all that class of invalids whose respiratory organs are deranged, may be benefited, and their lives prolonged, by a visit or residence in Minnesota, or the surrounding northern territory.

The present imperfect work is offered to the public, with the assurance that great benefit and pleasure can be obtained by an extended visit to Lake Superior, and the Upper Mississippi country, where abound game and fish in great quantities, and where the soil in most localities yields an abundant harvest of wheat and other kinds of grain.

Railroads are now being constructed diverging from St. Paul eastward, toward Chicago and Milwaukee, northward toward Lake Superior, the Upper Mississippi, and Red River of the North, and westward toward the Rocky Mountains—when completed, affording means for a speedy and extensive journey to the greatest health-restoring region of the world.

J. DISTURNELL.

New York, June, 1866.

ADVICE TO INVALIDS.

RESIDENTS of the Eastern or Southern States, seeking health or pleasure in the Upper Lake Region, or in the Upper Valley of the Mississippi, can proceed direct to Detroit or Chicago, from whence diverge Railroad or Steamboat Routes to every desirable point of the above extensive region of country.

From Cleveland and Detroit, Steamers run almost daily to Mackinac, Saut Ste. Marie, Marquette, and the different ports on Lake Superior. At all the above named places are well-kept hotels, and private boarding-houses, where quiet, together with pure water and invigorating air, can be enjoyed.

Starting from Chicago or Milwaukee, trains of cars run daily to Green Bay, Wis., connecting with Steamer and Railroad for Marquette, situated on the south shore of Lake Superior. Passenger trains also leave Chicago several times daily for Dubuque, Prairie du Chien, and La Crosse, connecting with a first-class Line of Steamers, running to St. Paul, Minn.

On arriving at Winona, Lake City, or St. Paul, an opportunity is afforded of a choice of hotels, or boarding-houses; the latter being more quiet and economical, and in many other respects preferable for invalids. The air and water alone, particularly in the Lake Superior region, seeming to afford vitality and eradicate many fatal diseases, so much so that the patient often is astonished at the sudden return of vigor and health. Their appetite, their strength, and enjoyment all often being restored as if by magic.

This beneficial effect is often produced in a few weeks' time, but, if months can be enjoyed in this health-restoring region, a perfect cure may be realized from many diseases.

For a permanent residence, the Upper Mississippi may be preferred, as there are more settlements and a wider range of habitable country to visit, abounding in lakes, surrounded by a rich agricultural region. The north shore of Lake Superior, attached to Minnesota, is of late attracting much attention, owing to its healthy climate and mineral wealth.

The months of July and August are the best time for invalids to start for Lake Superior or Minnesota, and they are advised to remain until September or October. The winter months, although cold, are passed with comparative comfort and benefit to those seeking permanent health.

J. D.

CONTENTS.

	PAGE.
THE UPPER MISSISSIPPI:—Its waters, tributaries, and extent of country drained—Population, etc.	9
Agricultural Productions, etc.—Table of Distances.	10
Railroad and Steamboat Routes from the City of New York to Lake Superior and the Upper Mississippi	11
Steamboat Route from St. Louis to Dubuque and St. Paul.	12
" " " St. Paul to Dubuque and St. Louis.	13
Distances from St. Louis to New Orleans—Steamboat Route from St. Paul to Mankato, Minn.	14
Railroads in Iowa, with their connections to Chicago.	15
Chicago to Rock Island and Council Bluffs—Chicago to Burlington, Iowa, etc..	16
CHICAGO, Description of.	17, 18
Railroads diverging from Chicago- -Railroad Route from Chicago to Dubuque	19
Elgin—Belvidere—City of Rockford, etc.	20
City of Freeport—Warren—Galena—Dunleith.	21
DUBUQUE, Description of.	22
Early History of Dubuque.	23
River Commerce of the West—Tonnage, etc.	24
Information for Travelers—Lines of Railroads running from Chicago.	25, 26
Railroad Route—Chicago to Dubuque.	27
Railroad and Steamboat Route—Chicago to Green Bay and Escanaba, Mich.	28
Railroad and Steamboat Route—Chicago to Green Bay and Lake Superior.	29
Juneau—City of Fond du Lac—City of Oshkosh—Lake Winnebago.	30
Neenah—Menasha—Appleton—Green Bay to Fond du Lac.	31
City of Green Bay—Fort Howard—Green Bay.	32
Green Bay to Escanaba and Marquette—Railroad and Steamboat Route.	33, 34
Railroad Route from Milwaukee to Madison and Prairie du Chien.	35
Chicago to Milwaukee, La Crosse, and St. Paul.	36
Railroad Route from Milwaukee to Madison and Prairie du Chien—City of Madison.	37
Railroad Route from Madison to Prairie du Chien—Elevation of several places above the Gulf of Mexico.	38
Railroad Route from Milwaukee to La Crosse, Wis.	39
Climate of Wisconsin.	40
Steamboat Excursion from Dubuque to St. Paul—Potosi—McGregor.	41
Prairie du Chien—Lansing—Brownsville.	42
City of La Crosse—Running of the Mississippi river by Moonlight.	43
La Crescent—Trempeleau—City of Winona	44
Winona and St. Peter Railway—Fountain City—Wabasha—Reed's Landing—Lake Pepin.	45

CONTENTS.

	PAGE.
Scenery above Winona on the Mississippi....	46
Maiden's Rock—Lake Pepin.......................	47
The Sun rising on Lake Pepin—Lake City...............	48
Red Wing—Prescott—St. Croix River—Steamboat Route—Hastings......	49
CITY OF ST. PAUL, description of.........................	50
Progress of Minnesota in Population and Wealth.................	51
St. Paul to St. Cloud, *via* Pacific Railroad—Early History of St. Paul......	52, 53
First Land Speculator in St. Paul—Jonathan Carver..................	54
Drive from St. Paul to the Falls of St. Anthony.....................	55
Mendota—Fort Snelling—Minnesota river........................	.56
St. Peter—Mankato—New Ulm—Buffalo Hunt......................	57
View of the Falls of St. Anthony............................	58
View of Minne-ha-ha—City of St. Anthony—Minneopolis................	59
Minne-ha-ha—Anoka—Big Lake—St. Cloud.......................	60
Sauk Rapids—Watab—Crow Wing—Northern Minnesota—Otter Tail Lake.	61
Interesting to Consumptives—Who should go to Minnesota and who should not...	62, 63
Railroads of Minnesota—Geological Survey........................	64
Steamboat Route from Chicago to Mackinac and the Saut Ste. Marie.......	65
Waukegan—Kenosha—Racine—Milwaukee.......................	66
Railroads running from Milwaukee—Granaries of Wisconsin and Minnesota.	67
Port Washington—Sheboygan—Manitouwoc—Kewaunee—Ahneepee, etc..	68
Manitou Islands—Fox Islands—Beaver Islands—Straits of Mackinac.......	69
MACKINAC—the Town and Fortress—Island of Mackinac.................	70
Lover's Leap—Altitude of various points on the Island...................	71
Arched Rock—Sugar Loaf—Purity of the Atmosphere.....................	72
Island of Mackinac—its romantic and picturesque appearance.............	73
Round Island—Point de Tour—Drummond's Island—St. Joseph's Island—Mud Lake..	74
Sugar Island—Lake George—Church's Landing—Garden River Settlement.	75
ST. MARY'S RIVER—Description of.................................	76
SAUT STE. MARIE—Fort Brady.....................................	77
View of the Falls and Rapids of Ste. Marie..........................	78
Portage Route from Lake Superior to Lake Winnepeg—Fort William—Kaministaquoiah River—Dog Lake.....................	79
Savan River—Rainy Lake—Lake of the Woods......................	80
Winnipeg River—Lake Winnipeg.................................	81
Lakes in the Valley of the Saskatchewan—Red River of the North........	82
Red River Settlement—Hudson Bay Company........................	83
Table of Distances—Fort William to Fort Alexander.....................	84

ADVERTISEMENTS..

Farming Lands of Illinois.

BEST FARMING LANDS IN THE WORLD!
For Sale by the Illinois Central Railroad Company,
In Tracts to suit Purchasers, AT LOW PRICES.

THE ILLINOIS CENTRAL RAILROAD COMPANY HAVE FOR SALE,
900,000 ACRES OF THE BEST FARMING LANDS IN THE COUNTRY.

The road extends from Dunleith, in the north-western part of the State, to Cairo, in the extreme southern part, with a branch from Centralia, one hundred and thirteen miles north of Cairo, to Chicago, on the shore of Lake Michigan—altogether a length of 704 miles—and the land which is offered for sale is situated upon either side of the track, in no instance at a greater distance than fifteen miles.

State of Illinois.

The rapid development of Illinois, its steady increase in population and wealth, and its capacity to produce cheap food, are matters for wonder and admiration. The United States Commissioner of Agriculture estimates the amounts of the principal crops of 1864, for the whole country, as follows: Indian Corn, 530,581,403 bushels; wheat, 160,695,823 bushels; oats, 176,690,064 bushels; of which the farms of Illinois yielded 138,356,135 bushels of Indian Corn ; 33,371,173 bushels of wheat ; and 24,273,751 bushels of oats—in reality more than one-fourth of the corn, more than one-fifth of the wheat, and almost one-seventh of the oats produced in all the United States.

Grain—Stock Raising.

Pre-eminently the first in the list of grain-exporting States, Illinois is also the great cattle State of the Union. Its fertile prairies are well adapted by nature to the raising of cattle, sheep, horses and mules ; and in the important interest of pork packing, it is far in advance of every other State. The seeding of these prairie lands to tame grasses for pasturage or hay, offers to farmers with capital the most profitable results. The hay crop of Illinois in 1864 is estimated at 2,166,725 tons, which is more than half a million tons larger than the crop of any other State, excepting only New York.

Inducements to Settlers.

The attention of persons, whose limited means forbid the purchase of a homestead in the older States, is particularly invited to these lands. Within ten years the Illinois Central Railroad Company has sold 1,400,000 acres, to more than 20,000 actual settlers ; and during the last year 264,422 acres —a larger aggregate of sales than in any one year since the opening of the road. The farms are sold in tracts of forty or eighty acres, suited to the settler with limited capital, or in larger tracts, as may be required by the capitalist and stock raiser. The soil is of unsurpassed fertility ; the climate is healthy ; taxes are low ; churches and schools are becoming abundant throughout the length and breadth of the State; and communication with all the great markets is made easy through railroads, canals and rivers.

PRICES AND TERMS OF PAYMENT.

The price of lands varies from $9 to $15 and upwards per acre, and they are sold on short credit, or for cash. A deduction of *ten per cent.* from the short credit price is made to those who buy for cash.

EXAMPLE:

Forty acres at $10 per acre, on credit ; the principal one-quarter cash down—balance one, two and three years, at six per cent. interest, in advance, each year.

	INTEREST.	PRINCIPAL.		INTEREST.	PRINCIPAL.
Cash Payment,		$100 00	Payment in two years,	$6 00	100 00
Payment in one year,	$18 00 12 00	100 00	" three years,		100 00

The Same Land may be Purchased for $360 Cash.

Full information on all points, together with maps, showing the exact location of Lands, will be furnished on application, in person or by letter, to

LAND COMMISSIONER, Illinois Central R. R. Co., Chicago, Illinois.

THE UPPER MISSISSIPPI.

The vast range of country drained by the Mississippi river proper, independent of its great tributary, the Missouri river, embraces most of the State of Illinois, and a great portion of the States of Missouri, Iowa, Wisconsin, and Minnesota; a small part of the waters of Illinois, on its northeast border, flows into Lake Michigan, while nearly one half of the waters of Wisconsin flow in the same direction, finding their outlet through the Great Lakes and the St. Lawrence river into the Atlantic Ocean. All the waters of Missouri and Iowa find their way into the Missouri or Mississippi river, and thence into the Gulf of Mexico. The waters of Minnesota in part flow northward, through the Red river of the North, into Lake Winnipeg, and thence into Hudson's Bay. A portion flows eastward into Lake Superior, whilst its most important streams are the Upper Mississippi, fed by numerous lakes, and the St. Peter's or Minnesota river, falling into the Mississippi a few miles below the Falls of St. Anthony.

The Mississippi river is navigable for steamers of a large class, during a good stage of water from St. Paul to St. Louis, a distance of about 800 miles, and from St. Louis to New Orleans at all seasons of the year, except when interrupted by ice, a further distance of about 1,200 miles; making an uninterrupted navigation, during most of the year, of upward of 2,000 miles, from the Falls of St. Anthony, to the Gulf of Mexico. It is also navigable for steamers of a small class for about 150 miles above the Falls of St. Anthony. The entire navigation of this great river and its numerous tributaries being estimated at 16,000 miles.

The Area and Population of the *five* States mostly drained by the Mississippi, are as follows:

	Area sq. miles.	Population, 1860.	Population, 1865.
Illinois	55,400	1,711,951	est. 2,000,000
Missouri	65,000	1,182,012	" 1,300,000
Iowa	55,000	674,913	754,732
Wisconsin	53,924	775,881	868,325
Minnesota	83,500	172,023	264,600
Total	312,824	4,516,780	5,187,657

This rich and fertile portion of the Union, when as densely populated as the State of New York, will contain about 25,000,000 inhabitants, and be capable of raising annually an immense amount of bread stuffs, meats, and other agricultural products for home consumption and foreign markets.

The following were the principal Agricultural products according to the United States Census of 1860.

	Bushels Wheat.	Indian Corn.	Oats.
Illinois	23,837,023	115,174,777	15,220,029
Missouri	4,227,586	72,892,157	3,680,870
Iowa	8,449,403	42,410,686	5,887,645
Wisconsin	15,657,458	7,517,300	11,059,260
Minnesota	2,186,993	2,941,952	2,176,002
Total	54,358,463	240,936,872	38,023,836

All this immense product, together with vegetables, beef, pork, and lumber, finds its outlet by means of the Mississippi river, the Lakes and St. Lawrence river, and the numerous Railroads running to Eastern markets.

The principal cities and centers of trade for the above States, lying on navigable waters, and from which Railroads diverge to different sections of the country, are St. Louis, Chicago, Milwaukee, Dubuque, and St. Paul. Between these different cities a healthy rivalry exists for the trade of this great North-Western region, which is annually increasing in population and wealth.

A large number of Steamers run between St. Louis, Dubuque, and St. Paul, stopping at intermediate landings, affording daily opportunities for travelers visiting the Upper Mississippi, now annually thronged with pleasure seekers and invalids in search of health.

Steamers, propellers, and sailing vessels run from Chicago, Milwaukee, and other lake ports on Lake Michigan, to Green Bay, Mackinac, Lake Superior, Detroit, Cleveland, Buffalo, and Lake Ontario, via the Welland Canal. These steamers and propellers are usually thronged with passengers during the summer months. Mackinac, Saut Ste. Marie, and the different ports on Lake Superior being delightful and healthy places of resort.

A Railroad and Steamboat route is now in operation, running from Chicago to Green Bay, and thence to Marquette, on Lake Superior, affording a speedy conveyance to this health restoring region. A Railroad is also in progress of construction to run from Bayfield, or Superior City, to St. Paul, Minnesota, which, when finished, will form one of the most desirable railroad and steamboat routes on the Continent of America—thus uniting the travel on the Mississippi, with the Great Lakes or Inland Seas of America, forming a line of travel from New Orleans to Lake Superior, and from thence to Montreal and Quebec, a distance of about 3,800 miles, or in other words, from the Gulf of Mexico to the Gulf of St. Lawrence.

TABLE OF DISTANCES,

From New Orleans to Quebec, via Lake Superior.

Cities, &c.	Miles.	Cities, &c.	Miles.
New Orleans	00	La Crosse, Wis.	1,853
Baton Rouge, La.	135	St. Paul, Minn.	2,060
Vicksburg, Miss.	387	Superior City	2,220
Helena, Ark.	715	Saut Ste. Marie	2,720
Memphis, Tenn.	800	Detroit, Mich.	3,093
Cairo, Ill.	1,020	Toronto, Can.	3,317
St. Louis, Mo.	1,247	Montreal	3,650
Dubuque, Iowa	1,707	**Quebec**	3,820

TABLE OF DISTANCES,

From the CITY of NEW YORK, to ST. PAUL, Minnesota, by the most DIRECT ROUTE.

CITIES, &c.	LINES OF TRAVEL.	Miles.
NEW YORK to ALBANY, via *Hudson River Railroad*		145
ALBANY to SUSPENSION BRIDGE, via *New York Central Railroad*		304–449
SUSPENSION BRIDGE to DETROIT, Mich., via *Gt. Western Railroad of Canada*		230–679
DETROIT to GRAND HAVEN, Mich., via *Detroit and Milwaukee Railroad*		189–868
GRAND HAVEN to MILWAUKEE, Wis., via *Steamboat Route across Lake Michigan*		85–953
MILWAUKEE to LA CROSSE, Wis., via *Milwaukee and St. Paul Railroad*		195–1,148
LA CROSSE to ST. PAUL, Minn., via *Steamboat Route on Mississippi river*		210–1,358

☞ Distance from BOSTON to ST. PAUL, via Detroit, etc., 1,403 miles.

Railroad and Steamboat Route,

From the CITY of NEW YORK to SUPERIOR CITY, WISCONSIN.

CITIES, &c.,	LINES OF TRAVEL.	Miles.
NEW YORK to DUNKIRK, via *Erie Railroad*		460
DUNKIRK to CLEVELAND, Ohio, via *Lake Shore Railroad*		143–603
CLEVELAND to DETROIT, Mich., via *Steamboat Route across Lake Erie*		120–723
DETROIT to PORT HURON, Mich., via *Steamboat Route*		73–796
PORT HURON to SAUT STE. MARIE, Mich., via *Steamboat Route crossing Lake Huron*		300–1,096
SAUT STE. MARIE to MARQUETTE, Mich., via *Steamboat Route crossing Lake Superior*		160–1,256
MARQUETTE to ONTONAGON*, Mich., via *Steamboat Route crossing Lake Superior*		220–1,476
ONTONAGON to BAYFIELD, Wis., via *Steamboat Route crossing Lake Superior*		78–1,554
BAYFIELD to SUPERIOR CITY, Wis., via " " " " "		80–1,634

The above *Great Railroad and Steamboat Routes*, extending from the Atlantic seaboard to the head of navigation on the Mississippi river, and to the head of Lake Superior, passing through Lake Huron, now forms two great lines of travel, East and West.

The Railroad lines from New York and Boston, to Chicago and Milwaukee, and to Prairie du Chien and La Crosse, lying on the east side of the Mississippi river, are running throughout the entire year, affording great facilities for passenger and freight traffic.

The Steamers on the Upper Mississippi, and on Lakes Huron and Superior, run for about seven months in the year, from May to the first of December, affording great facilities for the carrying of passengers and heavy freight.

These great through lines of travel connect with the *Grand Trunk Railway of Canada*, and with the *Pennsylvania Railroads*, all of which tend to give increased facilities to reach the head of Lake Superior and the Upper Mississippi, being on the direct route toward Montana, Idaho, Oregon, and Washington Territory—passing the Gold Fields lying contiguous to the Rocky Mountains.

---

*A Railroad is under construction to extend from Marquette to Ontonagon, a distance of about 120 miles, which will shorten the distance to the head of Lake Superior about 100 miles.

Steamboat Route from St. Louis to Dubuque and St. Paul

USUAL TIME, to DUBUQUE, 2¼ days; to ST. PAUL, 4½ days.   THROUGH FARE, $20.

Landings.	Miles.	Landings.	Miles.
St. LOUIS................	0	DUNLEITH, Ill.................	1–461
Mouth Missouri River..........	20	Potosi Landing, Wis..........	14–475
Alton, Ill.................	5—25	Buena Vista, Iowa............	15–490
Mouth Illinois River........		Cassville, Wis...............	4–494
Cap au Gris.................	40—65	Guttenburg, Iowa............	10–504
Clarksville, Mo..............	37–102	Clayton, Iowa................	12–516
Louisiana, Mo................	12–114	McGREGOR, Iowa..............	11–527
HANNIBAL, Mo................	30–144	**Prairie du Chien**, Wis..	3–530
QUINCY, Ill..................	20–164	☞ To Chicago, 229 Miles.	
Lagrange, Mo................	12–176	Lynxville, Wis...............	14–544
Canton......................	8–184	LANSING, Iowa...............	16–560
Alexandria, Mo...............	20–204	De Soto, Wis................	6–566
Warsaw, Ill..................		Victory, Wis................	10–576
Keokuk, Iowa.............	4–208	Bad Ax City, Wis....	10–586
Montrose, Iowa..	12–220	Brownsville, Minn............	16–602
Nauvoo, Ill..................	3–223	**La Crosse**, Wis...........	12–614
Fort Madison. Iowa..........	9–232	☞ To Milwaukee, 195 Miles.	
Pontoosuc, Ill...............	6–238	La Crescent, Minn...........	2–616
BURLINGTON, Iowa............	17–255	Richmond, Minn..............	16–632
OQUAWKA, Ill.................	15–270	Trempeleau, Wis.............	5–037
Keithsburg, Ill...............	12–282	**Winona**, Minn............	17–654
New Boston, Ill..............	7–289	Fountain City, Wis..........	12–666
MUSCATINE, Iowa.............	18–307	Mount Vernon, Minn..........	14–680
ROCK ISLAND, Ill. } DAVENPORT, Iowa }	30–337	Minneiska, Minn.............	4–684
		Alma, Wis...................	14–698
Le Claire, Iowa..............	18–355	WABASHA, Minn...............	10–708
Princeton, Iowa..............	·6–361	Reed's Landing...............	6–714
Camanche, Iowa..............	10–371	Foot Lake Pepin..............	2–716
Albany, Ill...................	3–374	North Pepin, Wis............	6–722
Clinton, Iowa................	6–380	LAKE CITY, Minn.............	5–727
FULTON, Ill. } LYONS, Iowa }	2–382	Maiden Rock, Wis............	8–735
		Frontenac, Minn..............	3–738
Sabula, Iowa.................	20–402	RED WING, Minn.............	18–756
SAVANNA, Ill.................	3–405	PRESCOTT, Wis...............	28–784
Bellevue, Iowa...............	23–428	Mouth St. Croix River.	
GALENA, Ill..................	12–440	Point Douglass, Minn..........	1–785
Dubuque, Iowa...........	20–460	HASTINGS, Minn..............	3–788
☞ To Chicago, 189 Miles.		**St. PAUL**, Minn...........	32–820

Steamboat Route from St. Paul to Dubuque and St. Louis,
CONNECTING with RAILROADS RUNNING to MILWAUKEE and CHICAGO.

Landings.	Miles.	Landings.	Miles.
St. PAUL	0	**Dubuque,** Iowa	1–360
HASTINGS, Minn	32	☞ To Chicago, 189 Miles.	
Point Douglass, Minn	3—35	GALENA, Ill	20–380
Mouth St. Croix River.		Bellevue, Iowa	12–392
PRESCOTT, Wis	1—36	Savanna, Ill	23–415
RED WING, Minn	28—64	Sabula, Iowa	3–418
Head Lake Pepin	2—66	LYONS, Iowa ⎱	20–438
Frontenac, Minn	16—82	FULTON, Ill. ⎰	
Maiden Rock, Wis	3—85	Clinton, Iowa	2–440
LAKE CITY, Minn	8—93	Albany, Ill	6–446
North Pepin, Wis	5—98	Camanche, Iowa	3–449
Reed's Landing, Minn	8–106	Princeton, Iowa	10–459
WABASHAW, Minn	6–112	Le Claire, Iowa	6–465
Alma, Wis	10–122	DAVENPORT, Iowa ⎱	18–483
Minneiska, Minn	14–136	ROCK ISLAND, Ill. ⎰	
Mount Vernon, Minn	4–140	MUSCATINE, Iowa	30–513
Fountain City, Wis	14–154	New Boston, Ill	18–531
Winona, Minn	12–166	Keithsburg, Ill	7–538
Trempeleau, Wis	17–183	OQUAWKA, Ill	12–550
Richmond, Minn	5–188	BURLINGTON, Iowa	15–565
La Crescent, Minn	16–204	Pontoosuc, Ill	17–582
La Crosse, Wis	2–206	Fort Madison, Iowa	6–588
☞ To Milwaukee, 195 Miles.		Nauvoo, Ill	9–597
Brownsville, Minn	12–218	Montrose, Iowa	3–600
Bad Ax City, Wis	16–234	**Keokuk,** Iowa	12–612
Victory, Wis	10–244	Warsaw, Ill	4–616
De Soto, Wis	10–254	Alexandria, Mo	
LANSING, Iowa	6–260	Canton, Mo	20–636
Lynxville, Wis	16–276	Lagrange, Mo	8–644
Prairie du Chien, Wis	14–290	QUINCY, Ill	12–656
☞ To Milwaukee. 194 Miles.		HANNIBAL, Mo	20–676
MCGREGOR, Iowa	3–293	Louisiana, Mo	30–706
Clayton, Iowa	11–304	Clarksville, Mo	12–718
Guttenburg, Iowa	12–316	Cap au Gris	37–755
Cassville, Wis	10–326	Mouth Illinois River	
Buona Vista, Iowa	4–303	**Alton,** Ill	40–795
Potosi Landing, Wis	15–345	Mouth Missouri River	5–800
DUNLEITH, Ill	14–359	**St. LOUIS**	20–820

TABLE OF DISTANCES
From St. Louis to New Orleans.

Landings.	Miles.	Landings.	Miles.
St. LOUIS, Mo............	00	Commerce, Miss..............	40–487
Jefferson Barracks............	12	Helena, Ark................	45–532
Herculaneum.................	18–30	Mouth of White River........	75–607
Selma, Mo...................	6–36	Napoleon...................	35–642
Ste. Genevieve...............	23–59	Gaines' Landing.............	40–682
Kaskaskia Landing, Ill........	6–65	Columbia, Ark..............	20–702
Mouth Kaskaskia River.......	15–80	Greenville..................	12–714
Chester, Mo.................	4–84	Port Worthington............	30–744
Grand Tower.................	46–130	Grand Lake, Ark............	5–749
Bainbridge...................	10–140	Ashton.....................	15–764
Cape Girardeau..............	15–156	Lake Providence, La.........	10–774
Commerce, Mo...............	16–172	Miliken's Bend..............	50–824
Cairo, Ill..................	35–207	**Vicksburg**, Miss...........	26–850
Columbus, Ken..............	18–225	Grand Gulf, Miss............	50–900
Hickman, Ken...............	25–250	Rodney, Miss...............	17–917
New Madrid, Mo.............	32–282	**Natchez**, Miss.............	60–977
Island No. 11................	5–287	Mouth Red River............	60–1,037
Needham's Cut-off...........	54–341	Bayou Sara, La..............	40–1,077
Plumb Point.................	20–361	Port Hudson, La............	11–1,088
Fulton, Tenn.................	10–371	**Baton Rouge**, La.........	24–1,112
Mouth of Hatchee River......	6–377	Plaquemine, La..............	25–1,137
Randolph....................	5–382	Donaldsonville, La..........	30–1,167
Memphis, Tenn............	65–447	**NEW ORLEANS**, La...	80–1,247

Steamboat Route from St. Paul to Mankato, Minn.

Landings.	Miles.	Landings.	Miles.
St. PAUL.................	0	**MANKATO**..............	0
Mendota.....................	5	**St. Peter**................	30
Fort Snelling................	1–6	Ottawa.....................	16–46
Credit River.................	10–16	Le Sueur...................	12–58
Bloomington.................	4–20	Henderson..................	10–68
Shakopee....................	12–32	Belle Plaine................	11–79
Chaska......................	6–38	St. Lawrence...............	6–85
Carver......................	4–42	Strait's Landing............	7–92
Louisville...................	4–46	Louisville..................	10–102
Strait's Landing.............	10–56	Carver.....................	4–106
St. Lawrence................	7–63	Chaska.....................	4–110
Belle Plaine.................	6–69	Shakopee...................	6–116
Henderson...................	11–80	Bloomington................	12–128
Le Sueur....................	10–90	Credit River................	4–132
Ottawa......................	12–102	Fort Snelling...............	10–142
St. Peter................	16–118	Mendota....................	1–143
MANKATO,..............	30–148	**St. PAUL**................	5–148

RAILROADS IN IOWA,
With their Connections to Chicago.

1. Chicago and North-Western, Dubuque and Sioux City, and Dubuque and South-Western Railway.

Stations.	Miles.	Stations.	Miles.
Chicago..................	0	Farley Junction............	23
Junction.....................	30	Dyersville.................	6—29
Elgin.......................	12—42	Earlville..................	8—37
Belvidere...................	36—78	Delaware...................	4—41
Rockford....................	14—92	Manchester.................	6—47
Freeport....................	29—121	Masonville.................	7—54
Dunleith....................	67—188	Winthrop...................	7—61
(*Mississippi river*.)		Independence...............	8—69
Dubuque, Iowa...........	0	Jesup......................	9—78
Julien......................	10	Raymond....................	9—87
Peosta......................	5—15	Waterloo...................	6—93
Epworth.....................	4—19	Cedar Falls................	6—99
Farley Junction.............	4—23	New Hartford...............	10—100
Worthington.................	7—30	Parkersburg................	9—119
Sand Springs................	7—37	Aplington..................	5—123
Monticello..................	6—43	Ackley.....................	9—132
Langworthy..................	4—47	**Iowa Falls**.............	11—143
Anamosa.....................	7—54	(*Stages.*)	
Viola.......................	7—61	Alden,	
Springville.................	4—65	Webster,	
Marion......................	8—73	Fort Dodge,	
Cedar Rapids................	6—79	**Sioux City** (*Missouri river*).	

2. Chicago and North-Western, Dixon Air Line and Iowa Division, Cedar Rapids and Missouri River Railway.

Stations.	Miles.	Stations.	Miles.
Chicago	0	Mount Vernon...............	9—203
Junction.....................	30	**Cedar Rapids**...........	16—219
Dixon.......................	68—98	Blairstown.................	24—243
(*Junction Illinois Central.*)		Belle Plaine...............	10—253
Fulton......................	38—136	Toledo.....................	17—270
(*Mississippi river*.)		Marshall...................	18—288
Clinton, Iowa...........	1—137	State Center...............	14—302
Camanche....................	5—142	Nevada.....................	17—319
Low Moor....................	5—147	**Boonsboro**..............	23—342
De Witt.....................	9—156	(*Stages.*)	
Wheatland...................	16—172	Jefferson,	
London......................	5—177	New Ida,	
Clarence	7—184	(*Missouri river.*)	
Mechanicsville..............	10—194	**Decatur,** Nebraska.	

3. Chicago and Rock Island, Mississippi and Missouri Railroads.

Stations.	Miles.	Stations.	Miles.
Chicago	0	Wilton	209
Joliet	40	Moscow	3—212
Ottawa	44—84	Atilissa	5—217
La Salle	15—99	West Liberty	5—222
(*Illinois river.*)		**Iowa City**	16—238
Bureau	15—114	Oxford	15—253
Rock Island	68—182	Marengo	16—269
(*Mississippi river.*)		Victor	12—281
Davenport, Iowa	2—184	Brooklyn	8—289
Walcott	12—196	Grinnell	15—304
Fulton	5—201	Kellogg	11—315
Durant	2—203		
Wilton	6—209		
Muscatine	13—222	(*Stages.*)	
Ononwa	12—234		
Clifton	10—244	**Des Moines,**	
Ainsworth	8—252		
Washington	7—259	**Council Bluffs.**	

4. Chicago, Burlington and Quincy, Burlington and Missouri Railroads.

Stations.	Miles.	Stations.	Miles.
Chicago	0	Danville	4—223
Aurora	40	New London	6—229
Mendota	45—85	Mount Pleasant	3—238
(*Illinois Central R. R.*)		Checauqua	7—245
Galesburg	80—165	Fairfield	15—260
Oquawka Junction	34—199	Whitfield	5—265
E. Burlington	10—209	Batavia	7—272
(*Mississippi river.*)		Agency City	7—279
Burlington, Iowa	1—210	**Ottumwa**	6—285
Middletown	9—219		

5. Des Moines Valley Railroad.

Stations.	Miles.	Stations.	Miles.
Keokuk, Iowa	0	**Ottumwa**	16—76
Sand Prairie	14	Eddyville	19—92
Belfast	6—20	Oskaloosa	7—101
Croton	5—25	Leighton	8—108
Farmington	5—30	Pella	8—116
Bentonsport	9—39	**Monroe**	14—130
Summit	6—45	(*Stages.*)	
Independence	14—59	**Des Moines.**	

CHICAGO,

"THE GARDEN CITY," the largest city of Illinois, is advantageously situated on the south-western shore of Lake Michigan, at the mouth of Chicago river, in N. lat., 41° 52', and W. long., from Greenwich, 87° 35'; being elevated eight to ten feet above the lake, the level of which great body of water is 578 feet above the Atlantic Ocean. This city has within thirty years risen from a small settlement around an old fort (Dearborn), to a place of great commercial importance, being now one of the largest interior cities in the United States, exhibiting a rapidity of growth and wealth never before known in the annals of the country. The harbor and river has a depth of from 12 to 14 feet of water, which makes it a commodious and safe haven; and it has been much improved artificially by the construction of piers, which extend on each side of the entrance of the river, for some distance into the lake, to prevent the accumulation of sand upon the bar. The light-house is on the south side of the harbor, and shows a fixed light on a tower 40 feet above the surface of the lake; there is also a beacon light on the end of the pier. In a naval and military point of view, this is one of the most important ports on the Upper Lakes, and should be strongly defended. Along the river and its branches, for several miles, are immense grain warehouses, some of which are capable of storing upward of 1,000,000 bushels of grain—and alongside of which vessels can be loaded within a few hours. The whole capacity for storage of grain exceeds 10,000,000 bushels. There are also immense storehouses for the storage of flour, beef, pork, whisky, and other merchandise, and capacious docks and yards for lumber, wood, coal, &c., Chicago now being one of the greatest grain, provision, and lumber markets in the world; the shipment of flour and grain alone, in 1865, being upward of 53,000,000 bushels.

The city of Chicago is laid out at right angles, the streets run from the lake westward, intersected by others, all of which are about 80 feet wide; it extends along the lake, north and south, about 8 miles, there being a gradual rise in the ground, affording a good drainage into the river and lake. The business portion of the city is mostly built of brick, and a fine quality of stone, sometimes called "Athens marble." This stone is found in the vicinity of the city, and is highly prized as a building material. The dwelling-houses are mostly constructed of wood, except costly residences, which are of brick, or stone and marble.

The city contains a United States custom-house and post-office building, a court-house and jail, the county buildings, a Marine Hospital, Rush Medical College, and Chicago Medical College; the Chamber of Commerce, a new edifice, built of Athens stone; a new opera house, academy of music, and other places of amusement; market houses; several large hotels; 120 churches of different denominations, many of which are costly edifices; 15 banks; 10 marine and fire insurance companies; gas works and water works. The manufacturing establishments of Chicago are numerous and extensive, consisting of iron foundries and machine shops, railroad car manufactory, steam saw, planing, and flouring mills, manufactories of agricultural implements, breweries, distilleries, &c. Numerous steamers, propellers, and sailing vessels ply between this place and the ports on Lake Michigan and Green Bay; also, to the Lake Superior ports, Collingwood and

Goderich, Can., Detroit, Cleveland, Dunkirk, Buffalo, and to the ports on Lake Ontario, passing through the Welland Canal vessels occasionally sailing to and from European ports, via the St. Lawrence river.

The *Illinois and Michigan Canal*, connecting Lake Michigan with Illinois river, which is 60 feet wide at the top, 6 feet deep, and 107 miles in length, including five miles of river navigation, terminates here, through which is brought a large amount of produce from the south and southwest; and the numerous Railroads radiating from Chicago add to the vast accumulation which is here shipped for the Atlantic sea-board. Chicago being within a short distance of the most extensive coal-fields to be found in Illinois, and the pineries of Michigan and Wisconsin, as well as surrounded by the finest grain region on the face of the globe, makes it the natural outlet for the varied and rich produce of an immense section of fertile country. The establishment of the great *Union Stock Yard*, during the past year, will render Chicago more attractive than ever as a cattle market. The receipts of beef cattle during the year ending March 31, 1866, amounted to 348,928; the total number of hogs, live and dressed, being 1,178,832; the receipts of lumber during the year ending March 51, 1866, amounted to 647,145,734 feet, against 501,592,406 feet received the preceding year. The *Lake Tunnel*, now in progress of construction, extending about two miles from shore under Lake Michigan, is intended to supply the city with pure and wholesome water. Two *Artesian Wells* are also in operation, situated three miles west of the lake, yielding 1,200,000 gallons of pure water daily. The *City Railroads* extend to the limits of the city in every direction, affording a cheap and speedy mode of conveyance, while, from the numerous railroad depots, passengers are conveyed to remote points, east, west, north, and south.

Number of Vessels arrived and cleared in 1865, with their Tonnage.

Total Vessels............ 10,067
Total Tonnage.......... 2,092,276

POPULATION OF CHICAGO AT DIFFERENT PERIODS.

United States Census, 1840.... 4,853
State Census, 1845........... 12,088
United States Census, 1850.... 29,963
State Census, 1855........... 80,000
United States Census, 1860.... 109,260
State Census, 1865........... 178,900

PRINCIPAL HOTELS IN CHICAGO.

NAME.	LOCATION.	PROPRIETOR.
Adams House,	Lake st. cor Michigan Avenue.	Pearce & Benjamin.
Briggs House,	cor. Randolph and Wells streets,	W. F. Tucker & Co.
City Hotel,	cor. Lake and Dearborn streets,	L. H. Ainsworth.
Matteson House,	cor. Randolph and Dearborn streets,	Robert Hill.
Metropolitan Hotel,	cor. Randolph and Wells streets,	B. H. Skinner.
Revere House,	cor. North Clark and Kinzie streets.	
Richmond House,	cor. South Water and Michigan Av.	R. Somers.
Sherman House,	cor. Randolph and Clark streets,	Gage, Waite & Co.
Stewart House,	cor. State and Washington streets.	
Tremont House,	cor. Lake and Dearborn streets,	Gage & Drake.

Chicago and North-Western Railway and its Branches.

		Miles.
1.	WISCONSIN DIVISION.—Chicago to Green Bay, Wis.	242
2.	MILWAUKEE DIVISION.—Chicago to Milwaukee, Wis.	85
3.	KENOSHA DIVISION.—Kenosha to Rockford, Ill.	72
4.	MADISON DIVISION.—Belvidere to Madison, Wis.	68
5.	PENINSULAR DIVISION.—Escanaba to Marquette, Mich.	68
6.	FOX RIVER VALLEY.—Elgin to Geneva Lake, Wis.	43
7.	GALENA DIVISION.—Chicago to Freeport, Ill.	121
8.	IOWA DIVISION.—Chicago to Jefferson, Iowa.	373

Total. 1,072

Other Railroads diverging from Chicago.

	Miles
Chicago and Rock Island	182
Chicago, Burlington and Quincy	275
Galesburg and Burlington Branch	45
Chicago, Alton and St. Louis	280
Illinois Central* (Chicago to Cairo)	365
Chicago and Great Eastern (Chicago to Cincinnati)	294
Pittsburgh, Fort Wayne and Chicago	468
Michigan Southern and Northern Indiana (Chicago to Toledo, Ohio)	243
Michigan Central (Detroit to Chicago)	284

Grand Total. 3,498

RAILROAD ROUTE,
FROM CHICAGO to GALENA, DUNLEITH, and DUBUQUE.

Passenger cars leave the Wells Street depot, Chicago, morning and evening, for Dunleith and Dubuque, connecting with STEAMERS running on the Mississippi river, and with the *Dubuque and Sioux City Railway.*

On starting from the depot, the Galena Division of the Chicago and North western Railway, runs west to the limits of the city, three miles, where may be seen, on the right hand, the celebrated ARTESIAN WELLS, and extensive ice house, where an immense volume of pure water is flowing continually, rising 25 feet above the earth's surface. Here are two wells, 700 feet in depth, yielding 1,200,000 gallons of water daily. In the winter season, the water is conveyed into extensive reservoirs, and suffered to congeal, producing ice of a good quality for city consumption and shipment.

The broad prairie land is next reached, skirted in the distance by a small growth of timber.

HARLEM, 9 miles from Chicago, is a small settlement, surrounded by oak and other prairie trees. The wide-spread prairie, with a rich growth of grass, and

---

* Main Branch, Dunleith to Centralia, 343 miles.

extensive corn-fields, next attracts the attention of the traveler.

COTTAGE HILL, 16 miles, is a small scattered settlement, surrounded by rich lands, under a high state of cultivation.

BABCOCK'S GROVE, 20 miles, is the name of a settlement surrounded by an extensive range of forest trees, through which the railroad track passes.

DANBY, 22¼ miles, is a small village, surrounded by a rolling prairie.

WHEATON, 25 miles, is a flourishing village, where is situated *Wheaton College*, several churches, stores, and manufacturing establishments.

WINFIELD, 28 miles, is surrounded by forest trees and prairie openings of small size.

JUNCTION, 30 miles. Here is a small settlement, and machine shops for railroad purposes. The *Chicago, Burlington,* and *Quincy Railroad* here diverges toward the Southwest, while the *Dixon and Iowa Division* of the Chicago and Northwestern Railway runs west to Fulton, situated on the Mississippi River. In this vicinity may be found the prairie hen, quail, snipe, plover, ducks, wild geese, and other game in their season, during the spring and fall months.

WAYNE, 35 miles, is a small railroad station.

CLINTONVILLE, 39 miles, is situated on Fox River, where are several flouring mills, propelled by water power.

Elgin, 42 miles from Chicago, situated on Fox River, is a large and flourishing town. Here are several flouring mills, a woolen factory, and other manufacturing establishments, propelled by water power. There is also an extensive watch manufactory, giving employment to several hundred workmen. Population, about 4,000. The *Fox River Valley Railroad* runs north from this place into Wisconsin, 43 miles, extending through a fertile section of country, which becomes somewhat hilly, with a fine growth of forest trees.

GILBERT'S STATION, 50 miles.

HUNTLEY, 55 miles, is a scattered village, surrounded by a rich section of country, where may be seen an extensive level prairie.

UNION, 62¼ miles, is a small, scattered settlement.

MARENGO, 66 miles, is a thriving village, where are several steam flouring and other mills.

GARDEN PRAIRIE, 72 miles, is a small village, surrounded by a fine section of country, producing corn and wheat in great abundance.

Belvidere, 78 miles from Chicago, is a large and flourishing village, situated on Kishwaukee river, flowing into Rock river. It is the capital of Boone County, and contains about 3,500 inhabitants. Here are two flouring mills and other manufacturing establishments, propelled by water power; several churches, hotels, and stores.

The *Beloit and Madison Railroad*, 68 miles in length, extends north through a fertile section of country.

CHERRY VALLEY, 84 miles, is situated on Kishwaukee river, which is here crossed by a long wooden bridge.

The City of **Rockford,** 92 miles from Chicago, and 96 from Dunleith, is advantageously situated on Rock river, where is a good water power. It is the capital of Winnebago County, and contains, besides the county buildings, fourteen churches, three national banks, several public houses, and numerous stores. There are several flouring mills, saw mills, a cotton factory, two woolen factories, and several other factories, employing water power. Population, about 10,000.

The *Kenosha Division* of the Chicago and Northwestern Railway terminates here, being 72 miles in length.

WINNEBAGO, 99 miles, is a small village.

PECATONICA, 106 miles, is a small settlement situated on a stream of the same name.

RIDOUT STATION, 114 miles.

The City of **Freeport,** 121 miles from Chicago, and 67 from Dunleith, the capital of Stephenson County, is favorably situated on Pecatonica river, being surrounded by a very fertile section of country. By means of a dam, a good water power is obtained, and used for propelling flouring mills, and other mills and factories. Here are ten churches, two banks, several hotels, numerous stores, and about 9,000 inhabitants. The *Western Union Railroad,* extending from Racine, Wis., to Savanna, on the Mississippi, runs through Freeport, where terminates the *Chicago and North-Western Railway;* the *Illinois Central Railroad,* running from Cairo, continues on to Dunleith.

ELROY, 129 miles, is a small village.

LENA, 134 miles, is a small place, surrounded by rich prairie lands.

NORA, 142 miles, is a small settlement.

WARREN, 145 miles from Chicago, is situated near the State line, which divides Illinois from Wisconsin, being 32 miles south of MINERAL POINT, which is the center of the lead region of Wisconsin. Warren is a flourishing place for trade, being surrounded by a rich agricultural and mineral section of country. Population, 2,500.

APPLE RIVER STATION, 151 miles. Here the country becomes rough and broken, surrounded by the lead region of Illinois and Wisconsin. Westward, the railroad passes through some deep cuts, and over high embankments.

SCALE'S MOUND, 160 miles, is a small settlement, surrounded by a hilly section of country, filled with lead mines.

COUNCIL HILL, 165 miles, is another small settlement, surrounded by lead mines, where excavations may be seen along the roadside. Westward the line of the railroad is very crooked, presenting some beautiful scenery as you approach Fevre River.

The City of **Galena,** 172 miles west of Chicago, the capital of Jo Daviess County, is an old and flourishing place of business, situated on Fevre river, six miles above its entrance into the Mississippi river. It is situated in a romantic ravine, and on hillsides of great natural beauty. Galena owes its importance, mainly, to the rich mines of lead with which it is surrounded, and possessing a secure harbor for steamers. Here are eight or ten churches, two banks, several hotels, numerous stores, and many fine private dwellings. Population, about 8,000. The trade of this city, formerly, was very extensive, but since the completion of the railroad to Dunleith, and access to Dubuque, it has, in part, lost its commercial importance, yet it is still a place of much wealth.

MENOMINEE STATION, 180 miles from Chicago, lies near the Mississippi River, where its waters are first seen flowing onward to the Gulf of Mexico.

Dunleith, Illinois, lies on the east bank of the Mississippi, here about half a mile in width, directly opposite Dubuque, by which it is connected by a steam ferry. The *Illinois Central Railroad* terminates here, running north from Cairo, 456 miles, thus forming, in part, a line of travel to Chicago, and a through line of travel to the mouth of the Ohio river. At Dunleith are a machine shop and foundry, an elevator for grain, a few stores and store-houses, public-houses and about 500 inhabitants.

DUBUQUE.

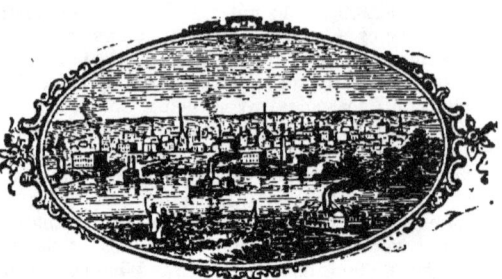

The City of **Dubuque** is advantageously situated on the west bank of the Mississippi river, here about half a mile in width, the bluffs being about one mile apart, in N. lat. 42° 30', W. long., 576 feet above the Gulf of Mexico. It stands on a plateau of ground, elevated about 20 feet above high water in the river, with bluffs rising to the height of 175 feet, which are of varied form, easy of access, and occupied by private residences, affording from their summits a fine view of the city and river. Dubuque was first settled in 1832, and incorporated as a city in 1847, being the county seat of Dubuque County. It is divided into five wards, and in 1865 contained a population of 15,814 inhabitants, and is rapidly increasing.

The city contains a United States Custom House, built of Nauvoo limestone, and accommodates the post office, the assessor and collector of the internal revenue for the third Congressional district, the office of the surveyor-general for Iowa and Wisconsin, and the clerk of the U. S. district court, and the court-room for said court; the county buildings, and a city hall, containing a general market, city court-room, room for the meeting of the city council, other offices for city purposes, and a large hall capable of seating 5,000 people; eighteen churches of different denominations; three public school buildings, attended by 600 pupils, a high-school building and several, primary school buildings; also, the Lee Seminary, a private school for young ladies; three national banks, and several private banks; a fire insurance company and numerous agencies; five hotels, and numerous stores and warehouses. Here are two large distilleries, six breweries, a brass and iron foundry, two flouring mills, five saw mills, a tub and pail factory, three sash, door and blind manufactories, a window shade factory, a threshing machine factory, a steam engine factory, two boiler factories, a car factory, and many other manufacturing establishments.

The *Dubuque and Sioux City Railroad* is now finished to Iowa Falls, 144 miles, and will soon be completed to Fort Dodge, 200 miles. When finished to Sioux City, on the Missouri River, a total distance of 325 miles, with its south-western branch to Cedar Rapids, it will afford great advantages to this portion of Iowa. A railroad is also being constructed from Cedar Falls to St. Paul, Minn., running in a northerly direction. Steamers of a large class form daily lines to St. Louis, on the south, and Prairie du Chien, and St. Paul, on the north, connecting with railroads running east and west.

HISTORY OF DUBUQUE.

DUBUQUE was the first place permanently occupied by white men in the State of Iowa. The first white persons who saw the beautiful prairie on which the city now stands were Father MARquette and his companions, connected with the Catholic Missions in Canada, and then upon a voyage for missionary purposes and exploration down the Mississippi. At that time—in the summer of 1673—heavy timber covered the bluffs, and scattering oaks grew upon the plateau now occupied by costly buildings. It was nearly a hundred years afterwards before trading posts were established on the Mississippi river, at Kaskaskia, St. Louis, and Prairie du Chien, and not until 1788, that JULIEN DUBUQUE, a Frenchman, obtained permission of the Sac and Fox Indians, in a council held at Prairie du Chien, to explore and work the lead mines in the vicinity of Dubuque. The same privilege was also granted to him in 1796 by Baron Carondolet, Governor of Louisiana, then a Spanish province, embracing all the land west of the Mississippi. He died in 1810, and was buried on the point of a steep bluff below the city.

The Upper Mississippi lead mines were first worked on the east side of the river by the Indians to furnish a means of commerce with the Indian traders. In 1823 they were worked by white men in the neighborhood of Galena, Ill.

The Black Hawk war commenced in 1831, and was closed in 1832. After the treaty made with the Sacs and Foxes, in the fall of the latter year, the Indians abandoned the place, the whites returned, and the first permanent settlement was made—the only one then in the territory west of the Mississippi, and north of the the State of Missouri.

At this time no part of Iowa had been obtained from the Indians. The country west of the Mississippi was a part of the "Louisiana purchase," obtained from the French government in 1803. That part of the territory, including what is now Iowa, was successively a part of the country attached to the Territory of Orleans, of Louisiana, of Indiana, and subsequently of Missouri until 1821.

After the admission of Missouri, in the last named year, the territory north of that State and west of the river—a part of which is now Iowa—remained unorganized, until settlements had been made on the west side of the river, and this region was attached to Michigan Territory in 1834.

In 1836, Iowa became a part of Wisconsin Territory, and was organized as Iowa Territory, in 1838. In 1847 it was admitted into the Union as a State.

The progress of Dubuque since 1838 may be inferred from the facts that the "corporation tax" of that year amounted to only $524, and in 1839 to $740, while the city tax levied in 1857 exceeded $113,000. The assessed value of the property in the latter year was nearly $14,000,000. From 1840 to 1850, the population increased from 1,000 to 4,071. The corporate limits then included one mile square. They have since, by an amendment made to the charter in 1852, been made to include about eleven square miles. The population, by a census taken in 1865, was 15,814.

The first permanent settlement in Iowa may be said to have been made here, and the appropriate name DUBUQUE given it by the sanction of a public meeting held in 1833, in honor of the name of its first settler, forty-five years before.

The land upon which the principal part

of the city is built is, upon an average, forty feet above the river, is mostly of a sandy and gravelly nature, and, therefore, generally dry. Few cities are so fortunate in relation to health. The ratio of deaths, to the whole number of inhabitants, appears, by the mortuary statistics for many years past, to be only about one in a hundred.

The climate of the whole of Iowa is represented as excellent; the air, especially on the prairies, being dry and bracing. The mean annual temperature varies from 46° to 52° Fahrenheit. The country generally, excepting the low margins of the rivers, is as free from epidemic diseases as the most favored portion of the Union.

The bluffs afford good quarries of building stone, and extensive brick manufactories are in operation within the city limits. A number of lumber yards and steam saw-mills are supplied by rafts of material from the pineries of Wisconsin and Minnesota.

One of the greatest sources of natural wealth in this vicinity are the inexhaustible mines of lead, yielding, even with the present imperfect mining, a product of nearly half a million dollars annually. The position of Dubuque, upon the Mississippi, nearly midway between St. Louis and St. Paul, about four hundred miles equi-distant, and also its location on the railroad lines across northern Illinois and southern Wisconsin, have made it the center of trade for this portion of the North-west. Sustained as the city is, by Railroads running west towards the Missouri river and the trade to a great extent, of the northern half of Iowa, and a part of that of Minnesota and western Wisconsin, and eventually of Nebraska and Dacotah, it is, no doubt, destined to become a large and important commercial metropolis.

The River Commerce of the West.

So much has been said heretofore of the immense Commerce of the Northern Lakes, and the River Commerce of the West, that it may be worth while to call attention to the following Tabular Statement, showing the amount of Tonnage belonging to the leading ports on the Mississippi river and its tributaries:

Custom Houses.	No. of steamers.	Registered tonnage.	Capacity in tons.	Value in dollars.
Cincinnati,	150	80,497 16	42,983	$4,134,000
Dubuque	20	3,204 37	5,137	459,500
Evansville	25	3,043 51	5,019	402,600
Galena	20	2,297 77	3,305	435,000
Keokuk	15	1,173 86	2,192	178,500
Louisville	66	14,100 64	25,425	1,994,500
Memphis	60	9,849 62	15,121	1,011,200
Nashville	12	1,183 06	2,156	108,000
New Orleans	80	15,860 07	21,625	1,292,000
Paducah	10	2,100 80	2,893	265,000
Pittsburgh	159	33,598 00	42,471	3,920,800
St. Paul	39	3,088 52	4,973	607,500
St. Louis	210	86,532 34	110,769	8,830,000
Wheeling	44	9,538 11	8,075	918,000
Total	910	216,067 83	292,144	$24,556,600

These figures are compiled from authentic records by a western official, and may be relied upon. They show that the war has not destroyed the commerce of the western rivers, as had been erroneously supposed. The great depots of this commerce are St. Louis, Pittsburgh, Cincinnati, New Orleans, and Louisville, in the order named. The pre-eminence of St Louis and Pittsburgh is owing to their being the terminal points of the water route of the great transit from the seaboard to the Mississippi. Beginning at Philadelphia, this transit reaches Pittsburgh by railroad, and there the water route begins. How vast this interest is, we see in the prosperity of the intermediate cities of Wheeling, Cincinnati, Louisville, and Evansville. Notwithstanding all that has been said of the miserable navigation of the Ohio, this table shows that the commerce of that river still remains the principal item in the trade of the West, despite all the rivalry of great lines of Railway.

INFORMATION FOR TRAVELERS.

THE following are the Lines of Railroad running North, North-west, West, Southwest, or South from Chicago, with the leading points to which they tend, or which are taken upon their course. These lines form the main arteries of the great Railway System of the West, of which Chicago may not be inaptly termed the heart, and they are cut and crossed in every conceivable direction by other roads, carrying the traveler to within a few miles of any point he may desire to reach. On many of these roads there is no second-class fare; we give it in all cases where tickets are issued at other than first-class rates:

1. The *Milwaukee Division* of the Chicago and North-Western Railway, skirts the western shore of Lake Michigan a distance of 85 miles, thence to La Crosse on the Mississippi river, via *Milwaukee and St. Paul Railway*, 280 miles, where it connects with Steamers for St. Paul and other points on the Upper Mississippi. The following are the Distances and Fares from Chicago:

	Miles.	1st Class.	2d Class.
Milwaukee	85	$3.00	$2.50
La Crosse	280	11.00	8.50
Winona	320	13.00	....
St. Paul	386	17.00	12.50

2. The *Chicago and North-Western Railway* [main line] runs from Chicago in a northwesterly direction to Janesville, a distance of 91 miles, and thence runs almost due north to the head of Green Bay, skirting the western shore of Lake Michigan at a distance of about 14 miles. The distance to Green Bay [Fort Howard] is 242 miles. Thence by Steamer to Escanaba is about 95 miles. This point is at the lower end of Green Bay whence to Marquette, on Lake Superior, is 75 miles. The following are the Distances of these points from Chicago with the Fares:

	Miles.	1st Class.
Janesville	91	$3.50
Fort Howard	242	8.75
Escanaba	337	10 00
Marquette	412	10.00

3. The *Galena Division* of the Northwestern Railroad runs due west from Chicago in a straight line to the Mississippi on the west border of the State of Illinois, at Fulton, a distance of 136 miles; thence to Boonesboro, more than half way across the State of Iowa, a further distance of 206 miles. At Boonsboro connections are made with Western stages for De Soto, Omaha, Council Bluffs, and Sioux City on the Missouri river.

Connections are also made at Fulton, with Steamboats plying between all points on the Mississippi river. The following are the Distances and Fares from Chicago:

	Miles.	1st Class.	2d Class.
Fulton	126	$5.43	$4.25
Boonsboro	342	14.80	....
De Soto	466	25.80	....
Omaha	500	30.50	....
Council Bluffs	490	30.00	....
Sioux City	520	31.80	....

4. The *Chicago and North Western Railway* also runs trains to, or connecting with, trains for Madison, Wisconsin, Prairie du Chien, and Dunleith, on the Mississippi.

	Miles.	1st Class.	2d Class.
Madison	138	$5.00	....
Prairie du Chien	229	9.00	$7.50
Dunleith	188	7.95	6.50
Dubuque (*by ferry*)	189	8.45	7.00

5. The *Chicago, Burlington and Quincy Railroad* runs from Chicago south-west by west to Galesburg, in the interior of the State, where it divides, one branch going to Burlington, and another to Quincy, both points lying on the Mississippi river. At Quincy it connects with the Hannibal and St. Joseph Railroad, which runs across the State of Missouri to the Missouri river, connecting at St. Joseph with packet lines to all points on the Missouri; also connects with stage lines to all the most important points west of the Missouri. The following are the Distances and Fares from Chicago:

	Miles.	1st Class.	2d Class.
Galesburg	165	$6.60	....
Burlington	210	8.00	....
Quincy	265	10.00	....
St. Joseph	471	21.50	$17.00

6. The *Chicago and Rock Island Railroad* runs across the State of Illinois, nearly due west from Chicago, to Rock Island, on the Mississippi river, and is continued in the Mississippi and Missouri Railroad to Kellogg, about half way across the State of Iowa, and the extension across the State to Council Bluffs and Omaha City is in progress [now supplied by stages]. The following are the Distances and Fares:

	Miles.	1st Class.	2d Class.
Rock Island	182	$7.30	$5.50
Kellogg	315	13.30	9.50
Council Bluffs	446	30.00	....

7. The *Chicago and St. Louis Railroad* runs through the State of Illinois in a south-west by south direction, taking a number of the most important towns on its course—as Bloomington and Springfield. It connects with Steamers to all points on the Mississippi and Missouri rivers. The Distances and Fares are as follows:

	Miles.	1st Class.	2d Class.
Bloomington	126	$5.70	....
Springfield	185	7.95	....
Alton	257	11.00	....
St. Louis	280	12.00	$10.00

8. The *Illinois Central Railroad* runs from Chicago nearly south to Cairo, at the junction of the Ohio and Mississippi rivers. At three-fourths of the distance thither, it joins at Centralia with the main line which runs from Centralia to Dunleith, taking a meridianal course right through the middle of the State. It connects at Cairo with Steamers to all points. The following are the Distances and Fares:

	Miles.	1st Class.
Centralia	253	$11.00
Cairo	365	15.00

RAILROAD AND STEAMBOAT ROUTE. 27

CHICAGO to DUNLEITH and DUBUQUE,

Via North Western Railway, connecting at Dubuque with the North Western Union Packet Line of Steamers running on the Upper Mississippi River.

Going West.			Officers.	Going East.		
Through Passenger Trains leave Chicago for Freeport and Dunleith at 9 A.M. and 10 P.M.			Wm. B. Ogden, *Pres.*, Chicago. Geo. L. Dunlap, *Supt.*, " B. F. Patrick, *Pass. Agt.*, "	Through Passenger Trains leave Dunleith for Freeport, Chicago, etc., at 5.15 A.M. and 4 P.M.		
Stations.	Miles.	Fare.	Connecting Lines.	Stations.	Miles.	Fare.
CHICAGO......	0	$ cts.	Railroads and Steamers.	DUBUQUE...	0	$ cts.
Harlem...........	9			Dunleith	0	
Cottage Hill......	16			Menominee.......	8	
Danby...........	23			Galena...........	17	
Winfield........	28			Council Hill	24	
Junction	30		Chicago, Burlington & Quincy	Scales Mound.....	29	
Wayne...........	35		Railway.	Apple River......	38	
Clintonville......	39			Warren...........	44	
Elgin............	42		Fox River Valley Railroad.	Nora............	47	
Gilbert's	50			Lena	55	
Huntley..........	55			Eleroy	60	
Union...........	62			Freeport........	68	
Marengo	66			(*Chicago & N. Western R.R.*)		
Garden Prairie....	72			Ridott...........	75	
Belvidere.......	78	3 15	Beloit and Madison Branch.	Pecatonica	83	
Cherry Valley ...	84			Winnebago.......	90	
Rockford.........	92	3 70	Kenosha & Rockford Railroad.	Rockford........	97	
Winnebago.......	99			Cherry Valley ...105		
Pecatonica 106				Belvidere.......111		
Ridott...........114				Garden Prairie...117		
Freeport........121		4 85	Illinois Central Railroad, running from Dunleith to Cairo.	Marengo.........123		
(*Illinois Central Railroad.*)				Union............127		
Eleroy 129				Huntley..........134		
Lena............134				Gilbert's.........139		
Nora............142				Elgin 147		
Warren..........145			Mineral Point Railroad, 32 miles in length.	Clintonville......150		
Apple River......151				Wayne 154		
Scales Mound.....160				Junction.........159		
Council Hill 165				Winfield.........161		
Galena..........172		7 30		Danby...........166		
Menominee......181				Cottage Hill 173		
Dunleith 189		7 95	Steamers on Mississippi River.	Harlem..........180		
DUBUQUE...		8 45	Dubuque and Sioux Railroad.	CHICAGO 189		

CHICAGO to GREEN BAY, Wisconsin,
Via Chicago and Northwestern Railway, connecting with Steamers for Lake Superior, etc.

Going North.	Officers.	Going South.
Through Passenger Trains for Green Bay and St. Paul, Minn., leave at 9 A.M. and 4.30 P.M.	Wm. B. Ogden, *Pres.*, Chicago. Geo. L. Dunlop, *Supt.*, " A. A. Hobart, *Asst. Supt.*, " B. F. Patrick, *Passr. Agt.*, "	Through Passenger Trains leave Green Bay for Chicago, etc., at 6.30 A.M. and 3.15 P.M.

Stations.	Miles.	Fare.	Connecting Lines.	Stations.	Miles.	Fare.
CHICAGO......	0	$ cts.	Railroads and Steamers.	GREEN BAY.	0	$ cts.
Des Plaines.....	16			Fort Howard...	1	
Dunton..........	22			De Pere.........	6	
Palatine.........	26			Wrightstown....	16	
Barrington......	31			Kaukauna.......		
Crystal Lake....	42		Fox River Valley Railroad.	Little Chute.....	25	
WOODSTOCK......	51			APPLETON........	28	
HARVARD.........	62	2 50	Kenosha and Rock River R.R.	Menasha.........	35	
Sharon, Wis.....	70			OSHKOSH.........	48	
CLINTON.........	78	3 15	Racine and Mississippi R. R.	Fond du Lac...	65	
Shopiere........	82			Oakfield.........	74	
Janesville......	91	3 50	Janesville Junction Railroad.	Chester..........	82	
MILTON JUNCTION..	99	3 80	Milwaukee & Prairie du Chien Railroad, for Madison, etc.	Burnett..........	90	
Fort Atkinson...	110			Minn. Junction...	94	
Jefferson........	116			Juneau..........	97	
Watertown......	130	4 75	Milwaukee & St. Paul R.R. for Portage City, La Crosse, etc.	Watertown.....	112	
Juneau..........	145			Jefferson........	125	
Minn. Junction..	148	5 00	Milwaukee and St. Paul R.R. for Beaver Dam, etc.	Fort Atkinson...	131	
Burnett.........	151			MILTON JUNCTION..	143	
Chester.........	160		Horicon Div. to Berlin, etc.	Janesville.....	151	
Oakfield........	168			Shopiere.........		
Fond du Lac...	176	6 25	Steamers on Lake Winnebago.	Clinton..........	164	
OSHKOSH.........	193	6 80	Steamers on Fox and Wolf Rivers, etc.	Sharon...........		
Menasha.........	206			Harvard, Ill.....	179	
APPLETON........	213	7 60		WOODSTOCK.......	191	
Little Chute....	218			Crystal Lake....	199	
Kaukauna.......	220			Barrington......	210	
Wrightstown....	226			Palatine.........	216	
De Pere.........	236			Dunton..........	220	
Fort Howard...	242		Steamers for Escanaba, Lake Michigan, etc.	Des Plaines.....	225	
GREEN BAY.		8 75		CHICAGO.....	242	

STEAMBOAT ROUTE
From Green Bay to Escanaba, Mich.

A Steamer runs daily, during the Season of Navigation, on the arrival of the Cars from CHICAGO, for ESCANABA, connecting with Cars on the *Peninsula Railroad*, for MARQUETTE—thus forming a Through Line of Travel from Chicago to Lake Superior.

RAILROAD AND STEAMBOAT ROUTE,

FROM CHICAGO to GREEN BAY and LAKE SUPERIOR, via the CHICAGO AND NORTH-WESTERN RAILWAY, connecting with the MILWAUKEE AND PRAIRIE DU CHIEN RAILWAY, and with the MILWAUKEE AND ST. PAUL RAILWAY.

ON leaving CHICAGO from Kinzie street depot, the railway runs direct over a level prairie, to DES PLAINES RIVER and STATION, 16 miles. Here is a beautiful growth of wood along the margin of the river, being the first passed.

DUNTON, 22 miles from Chicago, is a small village, surrounded by a fine section of country.

PALATINE, 26 miles, is finely situated on a rolling prairie, producing large crops of corn and wheat.

BARRINGTON, 31 miles, is another small village. Young timber, consisting of oak, poplar, basswood, and hickory, is seen in every direction, the land being hilly on approaching Fox river, where an iron bridge spans the stream.

CARY, 38 miles, is a small settlement.

CRYSTAL LAKE STATION, 42 miles, is one mile from the village and lake of the same name. A branch railroad runs to the lake, from which large quantities of ice are annually taken and carried to Chicago, the water being of a very pure quality.

WOODSTOCK, 51 miles, capital of McHenry county, is a flourishing village of about 1,500 inhabitants, being surrounded by a fertile section of country.

HARVARD, 63 miles, is a thriving village, where passengers usually stop for refreshments. The *Kenosha Railroad* crosses at this station, running west to Rockford, Illinois.

CLINTON JUNCTION, 78 miles. The WESTERN UNION RAILROAD, running from Racine, Wis., to Savanna, Ill., 142 miles, crosses at this station.

Janesville, 91 miles, is a flourishing city, capital of Rock County, Wis. It is finely situated on both sides of Rock river, 45 miles southeast of Madison, and 63 miles southwest of Milwaukee, by railroad. It contains a court house and jail, ten churches, several public houses, two national banks, and the State institution for the blind. Rock river here affords extensive water power, which is employed in mills and factories of various kinds, there being six flouring mills, two saw mills, two woolen factories, machine shops, foundries, &c. It was incorporated as a city in 1853, and contained in 1865 about 8,000 inhabitants.

MILTON JUNCTION, 99 miles. Here the *Chicago and North-Western Railway* unites with the *Milwaukee and Prairie du Chien Railway.* Passengers bound for Prairie du Chien run direct through Madison, Wis., to the Mississippi river, forming a favorite route of travel to Iowa and Minnesota.

FORT ATKINSON, 110 miles, is an old military post and settlement situated on Rock river.

JEFFERSON, 116 miles, the capital of Jefferson County, Wis., is a flourishing village, containing 1,600 inhabitants.

The City of **Watertown,** 130 miles north of Chicago, and 43 miles northwest of Milwaukee, with which it is connected by railroad, is a large and flourishing town, situated on Rock river, where is a good water power. It contained, in 1865, 6,682 inhabitants, being surrounded by a fertile and rich section of country. Here is the junction of the

Chicago and North-Western, and *Milwaukee and St. Paul Railways*, being distant 151 miles from La Crosse.

JUNEAU, 145 miles, is a small village, being the capital of Dodge county, named in memory of the first white settler of Wisconsin. Besides the county buildings, there are two churches, two hotels, and several stores.

MINNESOTA JUNCTION, 148 miles. Here a Railroad branches off to *Beaver Dam* and other stations northwest.

BURNET, 151 miles, is a small village situated on the west side of Horicon Lake.

CHESTER, 160 miles, is situated on the west side of Lake Horicon, which is about twelve miles long and six miles wide.

OAKFIELD, 168 miles is a small settlement.

Fond du Lac, capital of Fond du Lac County, is a flourishing city, favorably situated at the head of Lake Winnebago, 87 miles N. N. W. from Milwaukee, and 176 miles from Chicago, by the *Chicago and North-Western Railway*, now finished through to Green Bay, a total distance of 242 miles. Here are located the county buildings, ten churches, four banks, six public-houses, 100 stores of different kinds, a steam grist mill, ten steam saw mills, a steam car factory, steam engine manufactory, machine shops, and various other manufacturing establishments. Population, 11,000. The lumber and produce business is very extensively carried on here, affording profitable returns. Fond du Lac is celebrated for its *fountains*, water being found of a pure quality by means of Artesian Wells, in which the city abounds.

The City of **Oshkosh,** 193 miles from Chicago, lying on the west side of Lake Winnebago, 20 miles north of Fond du Lac, is a large and flourishing place, being favorably situated at the mouth of Fox river on both sides of the stream. It now contains an active population of about 9,000 inhabitants. From its wharves steamers run to all the ports on the lake and Fox river, while the *Chicago and North-Western Railway* extends northward to Green Bay. It contains the county buildings, ten churches, several well-kept hotels, 100 stores of different kinds, besides steam grist mills, steam saw mills, iron foundries, cabinet shops, and a great number of other manufacturing establishments. This is a great mart for lumber, being brought down the Fox or Wolf river for upwards of 100 miles, this stream flowing through a fine *pine region* of country, for which northern Wisconsin is justly celebrated.

LAKE WINNEBAGO is a most beautiful sheet of water, being 32 miles long and about 12 miles wide, with bold land on the east shore, while on the west it seems elevated but a few feet above the waters of the lake. It abounds with several varieties of fish, of a fine flavor, affording rare sport to the angler. Steamers run through the Upper Fox or Wolf river, emptying into the lake at Oshkosh, for upwards of 100 miles, bringing down immense quantities of lumber, and agricultural products.

The *Fox River Improvement* is a work of great magnitude, affording by means of locks and dams a water communication from Green Bay to Lake Winnebago, and thence south-westward through the Upper Fox river to Portage City, where, by means of a canal, it interlocks with the Wisconsin river, falling into the Mississippi at Prairie du Chien.

This enterprise is thus graphically described:

"'MEETING OF THE WATERS.'—A gentleman, recently from Green Bay, mentioned a curious fact a day or two since, illustrative of the results of the completion of the River Improvement. He saw lying at the docks in that place the steamer *Appleton Belle*, built at Pittsburgh, and the steamer *Gurdon Grant*, built at Philadelphia—points on opposite sides of the Alleghany Mountains, and on waters flowing on one hand to the Atlantic, and on the other to the Mississippi and Gulf of Mexico. The *Belle* had sailed northward and westward through the Ohio, Mississippi, and Wisconsin; and the *Grant* in a contrary direction through the Delaware and Hudson, along the Erie Canal, and the chain of the Great Lakes. These are the victories of commerce, in which Wisconsin is playing a prominent part."

NEENAH, lying at the foot of Lake Winnebago, on the west shore, is a flourishing village of about 2,500 inhabitants.

MENASHA, 35 miles from Green Bay, is situated on an expansion of the river, here called *Lake Butte des Morts*, where is a lock and a canal of about one mile in length. Here are several large manufacturing establishments, and a population of about 2,000.

APPLETON, Outaganie Co., Wis., 213 miles from Chicago, is situated on Fox or Neenah river, 30 miles from its entrance into Green Bay, and five miles from Lake Winnebago, where are rapids called the *Grand Chute*. The river descends here about 30 feet in one mile and a half, affording an inexhaustible amount of water-power. Here are located three flouring mills, six saw mills, and several other extensive manufacturing establishments. This is the capital of the county, where is situated the *Lawrence University;* and it is no doubt destined to become a large manufacturing and commercial place, from the facilities which it possesses, by means of navigation and hydraulic power. Population, 3,000. Steamers run south into Lake Winnebago, and north into Green Bay.

The approach to Appleton from Green Bay, by water, is most lovely and picturesque—the river here winding through a rich section of country, clothed for several miles by a dense forest, extending to the very margin of the water. During the early autumn months, the scene is truly gorgeous, the foliage presenting every variety of color.

LITTLE CHUTE, 25 miles from Green Bay, is a small French settlement, where is an old Roman Catholic Mission House. Here are four locks, there being a descent of 40 feet in the river.

KAUKAUNA, 4 miles further, is a small village. Here are five locks, overcoming a fall of 60 feet.

WRIGHTSTOWN, 16 miles from Green Bay, is a small settlement, where is a steam saw mill and other manufacturing establishments.

LITTLE KAUKAUNA, here is a fall of 8 feet, with lock and dam.

DE PERE, 6 miles above Green Bay, is a town of about 700 inhabitants, where is a fall of 8 feet, also a lock for the passage of steamers.

Green Bay to Fond du Lac, Wisconsin.

There is now a railroad and steamboat route, extending from Green Bay to Appleton, Oshkosh, and Fond du Lac, situated at the head of Lake Winnebago, 60 miles distant, the latter passing through Fox river and the above beautiful sheet of water.

Fox, or NEENAH RIVER rises in Marquette Co., Wis., and, passing through Lake Winnebago, forms its outlet. This important stream is rendered navigable for steamers of a small class by means of dams and locks, forming, in connection with a short canal to the Wisconsin river, a direct water communication from Green Bay to the Mississippi river, a distance of about 200 miles. The rapids in the lower part of Fox river afford an immense water-power, while the upper section of country through which it flows, produces lumber and grain in great abundance. Here is a fall of 170 feet in the distance of 35 miles, after leaving Lake Winnebago.

The City of **Green Bay**, and capital of Brown Co., Wis., is favorably situated at the head of Green Bay, where enters the Lower Fox and East rivers, both being navigable for a few miles, the former being improved, by means of locks and canals, so as to form a navigable communication with Lake Winnebago and the Upper Fox river, connecting by means of a canal, 1¼ miles in length, with the Wisconsin river, emptying into the Mississippi at Prairie du Chien. It is thus on the line of water communication between the Gulf of Mexico and the Gulf of St. Lawrence. The capacity of the harbor is unequalled, there being a sufficient depth of water to admit vessels of a large size, and room to accommodate all the shipping of the Upper Lakes. The *Chicago and North-Western Railway* terminates at Fort Howard, opposite Green Bay, being 242 miles in length, uniting with lines of travel through Wisconsin, and connecting at its terminus with lines of Steamers running to Escanaba, Mackinac, and other ports of Canada and the United States. A railroad is proposed to be built to run from Green Bay to St. Paul, Minn., and another to run north to Escanaba—thus making a direct railroad communication from Milwaukee and Chicago, to Lake Superior. This latter route has become a favorite pleasure trip, connecting at Green Bay with a daily line of Steamers running to Escanaba, Mich., there again connecting with the *Peninsular Railroad*, running to the Iron and Copper mines of Lake Superior.

A free drawbridge connects Green Bay with *Fort Howard*, where is located the railroad depot, the river here being about one third of a mile in width. Docks are erected on both sides of the stream for the accommodation of vessels.

The city of *Green Bay* and *Fort Howard*, united, contain a population of about 4,000 inhabitants, their interest being closely identified. Here are congregated ten churches, two national banks, ten hotels, fifty or sixty stores and warehouses, two elevators, one steam grist mill, steam saw mills, one iron foundry and machine shop, one ship yard for building steamers, &c.

The water power of Fox river, it having a descent of 170 feet below Lake Winnebago, affords advantages unsurpassed for milling and manufacturing purposes. At *De Pere*, 5 miles above Green Bay, where lake navigation ceases, there being a fall of 12 feet in the river, are located numerous mills and manufacturing establishments, the water-power being as yet but partially improved, affording room for other establishments.

GREEN BAY, about 100 miles long and from 20 to 30 miles wide, is a splendid sheet of water, destined no doubt to be enlivened with commerce and pleasure excursions. Here are to be seen a number of picturesque islands and headlands. Several important streams enter into Green Bay, the largest of which is Neenah or Fox river, at its head, and is the outlet of Winnebago Lake. Menomonee river forms the boundary between the States of Wisconsin and Michigan, and empties into the bay opposite Green Island.

The recent improvement of the Fox and Wisconsin rivers not only opens steamboat navigation between the Bay and the head of Lake Winnebago, but it connects the Fox and Wisconsin rivers, one of which, flowing northward, falls into the Atlantic through the St. Lawrence, and the other, running southward, discharges its waters, through the Mississippi, into the Gulf of Mexico. By this connection a steamer can start from New Orleans, pass up the Mississippi to the mouth of the Wisconsin, pass up this river to Portage, through a short canal to the Upper Fox river, down this river to Lake Winnebago, at Oshkosh— down the lake to the point where it contracts into the Lower Fox—down this romantic river some thirty-five miles, by means of numerous canals around the principal rapids, into Green Bay, and so on without interruption through the great lakes into the St. Lawrence to the Atlantic Ocean.

GREEN BAY to ESCANABA and MARQUETTE,
By Steamer and Railroad Route.

On leaving the City of Green Bay in one of the steamers of the Green Bay Transit Company for Escanaba, 100 miles, you pass through one of the most beautiful sheets of water, connecting with Lake Michigan on the north.

The harbor of Green Bay is formed by the Fox or Neenah river, which here enters from the south, the outward channel being crooked and circuitous until the Light-house, 7 miles distant, is passed, when the bay widens, and a large expanse of water is presented to view.

Oconto, 30 miles north of Green Bay, having daily communication by steamboat, is a flourishing lumbering village lying on the west side of the bay, at the mouth of a river of the same name.

Little Sturgeon Point, 40 miles, lies on the east shore.

Sturgeon Bay is a deep indentation, running nearly across the neck of land which separates Green Bay from Lake Michigan, where it is proposed to construct a ship canal.

Menomonee, 58 miles, lies at the mouth of the river of the same name, which divides the States of Wisconsin and Michigan. This is a large and flourishing lumbering village, from where are annually shipped large quantities of lumber to Chicago, and eastern markets.

Green Island, 60 miles, being halfway to Escanaba, lies in the middle of the bay, where is a light-house to guide the mariner.

Hat Island and Strawberry Island are small bodies of land passed on the east, near the main shore.

Chamber's Island, 75 miles, is a large and fertile body of land, lying near the middle of the bay, here being about 20 miles wide.

Port des Morts, or Death's Door, is the entrance into Lake Michigan, separating the main land from Washington Island, on the north, which is attached to the State of Michigan. To the east lie the broad waters of Lake Michigan.

Cedar River, 90 miles, enters from the west, where is a lumbering establishment, the whole west shore of Green Bay producing a large growth of pine and other kinds of timber.

The Steamer now runs direct for *Little Bay de Noquet*, 30 miles distant, affording a view of the waters of Lake Michigan on the east, while to the north lies *Great Bay de Noquet*, about 10 miles wide and 20 miles in length.

PENSAUKEE, PESHTIGO, and other towns are springing up on the west shore of Green Bay, where are to be found numerous large lumber establishments, situated on the streams running into the bay.

ESCANABA, Delta Co., Michigan, is a new and promising town, situated on the western shore of Little Bay de Noc, 120 miles north of the city of Green Bay, and is the southern terminus of the *Peninsula Railroad of Michigan*. This place, laid out in the Spring of 1864, has commanding advantages, where is a good and secure harbor, of easy access, with a sufficient depth of water for the largest class of vessels navigating the lakes. The docks erected by the railroad company are of a substantial and commodious character, intended for the transhipment of iron and copper ore from the Lake Superior mines, distant about 65 miles.

The site of the town lies on Sand Point, where is a favorable view of the waters of Green Bay lying to the south, and Little Bay de Noc on the north. The streets are laid out at right angles, with ample public grounds adjoining the waterfront. Stores and warehouses are about being erected, also a church, and a first-class hotel. The future of this place is hard to predict, its growth being identified with the rich mineral deposits of the Upper Peninsula of Michigan, bordering on Lake Superior.

The *Peninsular Ralroad* runs from the wharf at Escanaba, through a new and wild section of country to Negonnee, 62 miles, there intersecting the *Bay de Noquet and Marquette Railroad*, 14 miles above Marquette, forming a through line of travel.

The *Bay de Noquet and Marquette*, and the *Marquette and Ontonagon Railroads*, form a connection at the iron mines, and now extend to Lake Michigommi, 40 miles from Marquette. This important road will be extended to Ontonagon, 120 miles, also, to Portage Lake, thus connecting the iron and copper regions of Lake Superior.

MILWAUKEE TO MADISON & PRAIRIE DU CHIEN,

VIA MILWAUKEE AND PRAIRIE DU CHIEN RAILWAY, CONNECTING WITH STEAMERS FOR ST. PAUL, MINN.

Going West.	Officers.	Going East.
Through Passenger Trains leave Milwaukee at 11 A.M. and 6 P.M.	L. H. MEYER, *Pres.*, N. York. S. S. MERRILL, *Gen. Man.*, Milwaukee. A. REASONER, *Supt.*, "	Through Passenger Trains leave Prairie du Chien at 7.15 A.M. and 4 P.M.

STATIONS.	Miles.	Fare.	Connecting Lines.	STATIONS.	Miles.	Fare.
Milwaukee	0	$ cts.	Railroads and Steamers.	**Prairie du Chien**	0	$ cts.
Elm Grove	10			Lower Town	2	
JUNCTION	14		Milwaukee and St. Paul R. R., for Watertown, Portage City, La Crosse, etc.	Bridgeport	8	
Waukesha	20			Wauzeka	18	
Genesee	28			Woodman	22	
Eagle	36			Boscobel	28	
Palmyra	42			Muscoda	43	
WHITE WATER	50			Avoca	49	
Milton	62			Lone Rock	55	
Milton Junc.	63		Chicago and Northwestern R. R., running from Chicago to Green Bay, etc.	Spring Green	62	
Edgerton	70			Arena	69	
Stoughton	80			Mazomanie	75	
McFarland	89			Black Earth	79	
Madison	95		Beloit and Madison R. R.	Cross Plains	84	
Middleton	102			Middleton	92	
Cross Plains	110			**Madison**	98	
Black Earth	115			McFarland	105	
Mazomanie	118			Stoughton	113	
Arena	124			Edgerton	123	
Spring Green	132		Wisconsin River.	Milton Junction	130	
Lone Rock	138			Milton	132	
Avoca	145			WHITE WATER	143	
Muscoda	151			Palmyra	152	
Boscobel	165			Eagle	157	
Woodman	171			Genesee	165	
Wanzeka	176			Waukesha	173	
Bridgeport	186		Mississippi River & McGregor Western R. R. Steamers for St. Paul, etc.	JUNCTION	180	
Lower Town	192			Elm Grove	184	
Prarie du Chien	194			**Milwaukee**	194	

☞ The MILWAUKEE and PRAIRIE DU CHIEN RAILWAY, in connection with the DETROIT and MILWAUKEE RAILROAD, and other Railroads, form a direct Line of Travel from the Eastern States and Canada, to the Mississippi River.

CHICAGO to MILWAUKEE, LA CROSSE & ST. PAUL

Via Chicago and Milwaukee, and Milwaukee and St. Paul Railroads.

Going North.	Officers.	Going South.
Through Passenger Trains leave Chicago for Milwaukee, &c., at 9 A.M. and 4.20 P.M.	Geo. L. Dunlap, *Supt.*, Chicago A. Reasoner, *Supt.*, Milwaukee D. A. Olin, *Asst. Supt.*, "	Through Passenger Trains leave La Crosse for Milwaukee, etc., at 5 A.M. and 1 P.M.

Stations	Miles.	Fare.	Connecting Lines.	Stations.	Miles.	Fare.
CHICAGO	0	$ cts.	Railroad and Steamers.	LA CROSSE	0	$ cts.
Rosehill	8			West Salem	11	
Evanstown	12			Sparta	25	
Winnetka	16			Greenfield	39	
Glencoe	19			Lisbon	63	
Highland Park	23			Manston	68	
Lake Forrest	28			Kilbourn City	90	
Rockland	30			Portage City	104	
Waukegan	35			Columbus	132	
State Line	45			Watertown	152	
Kenosha, Wis.	52		Kenosha and Rockford R. R.	Oconomowoo	164	
Racine Junction	60			Milwaukee	195	
Racine	62		Racine and Mississippi R. R.	Depart, 3.70 A.M. & 4.30 P.M.		
Oak Creek	76			(*Chicago & Milwaukee R.R.*)		
Milwaukee	85	3 00	Railroads and Steamers.	Oak Creek	204	
Depart 1.40 and 8.30 P.M.				Racine	218	
(*Milwaukee & St. Paul R.R.*)				Racine Junction	220	
Oconomowoo	116			Kenosha	228	
Watertown	128	4 75	Chicago & NorthWestern Railway running to Green Bay. Wisconsin River.	State Line	235	
Columbus	148	5 75		Waukegan, Ill.	245	
Portage City	176	6 80		Rockland	250	
Kilbourn City	190	7 50		Lake Forest	252	
Manston	212			Highland Park	257	
Lisbon	217	8 60		Glencoe	261	
Greenfield	241			Winnetka	264	
Sparta	255	10 00		Evanston	268	
West Salem	269			Rosehill	272	
LA CROSSE	280	11 00	Steamers on the Mississippi running to St. Paul.	CHICAGO	280	11 00
Arrive,				*Arrive,*		

STEAMBOAT ROUTE
From La Crosse to St. Paul, Minn.

On the arrival of Through Trains at La Crosse, from Chicago and Milwaukee, passengers are immediately conveyed by Steamers, running on the Mississippi River, to St. Paul and all the intermediate landings—affording the most direct and speedy route to the Upper Mississippi.

RAILROAD ROUTE from MILWAUKEE to MADISON and PRAIRIE du CHIEN.

This popular and direct route of travel, running from Lake Michigan to the Mississippi river, runs for the most part through a rich agricultural section of country, passing through several important cities and villages.

At the JUNCTION, 14 miles, the *Milwaukee and Watertown Division* of the Milwaukee and St. Paul Railway diverges towards Watertown, forming a line of travel to La Crosse and St. Paul.

WAUKESHA, 20 miles, is a flourishing village, and the capital of Waukesha county, situated on Fox river. The court-house and jail are built of a fine quality of limestone, quarried in the immediate vicinity. There are 5 churches, 2 banks, an institution styled Carroll College, several public houses, a flouring mill, iron foundry, a machine shop and car factory. The population of the village is about 3,000.

WHITE WATER, 50 miles, is a thriving village, situated on an affluent of Rock river, where is a good water power. Here are 5 churches, 2 banks, flouring mills, a paper mill, and other manufacturing establishments. The population in 1860 was 2,731.

MILTON JUNCTION, 63 miles, is situated 99 miles north of Chicago. Here crosses the *Chicago and North-Western Railway*, running to Green Bay, 143 miles distant.

The Railroad route from Milton Junction to Madison, 32 miles, runs through a good section of country, where lie several beautiful bodies of water, forming the head sources of Rock river, which river in its course to the Mississippi drains the finest portions of Wisconsin and Illinois.

RAILROAD ROUTE CONTINUED—CHICAGO AND MILWAUKEE TO ST. PAUL.

The City of **Madison,** the capital of the State of Wisconsin, and seat of justice of Dane co., is delightfully situated on an isthmus between Lakes Mendota and Monona, 95 miles, by railroad route west of Milwaukee, and 132 miles north-west of Chicago, in lat. 43° 5′ north, long. 89° 20′ west, being elevated 256 feet above Lake Michigan, and 843 feet above the Atlantic ocean. The new capitol is a beautiful structure, standing 70 feet above the level of the surrounding lakes, and in the centre of a public park adorned with beautiful forest trees. The University of Wisconsin, which was instituted in 1849, stands on an eminence one mile west of the capitol, on ground elevated about 125 feet above the lakes. The Wisconsin Historical Society is a flourishing and highly useful institution. It possesses a rare library of choice books and many fine specimens of great interest. The city contains 12 churches, 4 banks, 4 hotels, 75 stores, a woolen factory, 2 iron foundries, several steam mills, and other manufacturing establishments. It contained, in 1865, 9,191 inhabitants.

Here are four beautiful lakes in the immediate vicinity of the city: Lake Mendota, the largest, which lies on the north side, is 6 miles long by 4 miles wide, being a lovely sheet of water, with clean, gravelly shores and bold banks. Lake Monona is rather smaller, and floats a small steamer, which affords a most delightful excursion around the lake.

This beautiful city and its vicinity is much frequented by pleasure seekers as a place of summer resort. The author of "Western Portraiture" gives the following lively sketch of this place and its environs: "Madison perhaps combines and overlooks more charming and diversified scenery to please the eye of fancy and promote health and pleasure than any town in the West; and in these respects it surpasses every other State capital in the Union. Its bright clear lakes, fresh groves, rippling rivulets, shady dales, and flowery meadow lawns, are commingled in greater profusion and disposed in more picturesque order than we have ever elsewhere beheld. Nor is it less noteworthy for its business advantages and its healthy position."

The railroad route west of Madison passes through a broken and hilly section of country producing large crops of wheat and other kinds of grain, although not so thickly settled as the more favored portions of the State.

Moso-Maine, 23 miles from Madison, is a thriving village, surrounded by a good section of country, which becomes more sandy as you proceed westward, toward the valley of the Wisconsin river.

At Helena, 35 miles west of Madison, the railroad track crosses the Wisconsin river, here about one-third of a mile in width. This stream is navigable for a small class of steamers from its mouth to Portage City, where is constructed a canal, uniting with Fox river, which empties into Winnebago Lake, thus forming a water communication, when the river is high, from the Mississippi river to Green Bay, and thence into Lake Michigan.

The *Milwaukee and Prairie du Chien Railroad* continues on the north side of Wisconsin River, passing through its valley, which is fringed with hills or bluffs in many places, the soil being sandy and rather unproductive.

Boscobel, 70 miles west of Madison, is a flourishing village, situated on the river. Other small villages are passed before reaching Prairie du Chien, which is divided into two villages or settlements. A steam ferry crosses the Mississippi from Lower Prairie du Chien to McGregor, Iowa.

For a description of Prairie du Chien, see p. 42.

Table, showing the Elevation of several Places above the Gulf of Mexico.

	Feet.		Feet.
Cairo, Illinois	275	Crow Wing, Minn	1,100
St. Louis, Missouri	335	Itasca Lake, Minn	1,550
Alton, Illinois	246		
Rock Island, Illinois	528	Lake Michigan, at Chicago, Ill.	578
Dubuque, Iowa	576	Lake Winnebago, Wisconsin	748
Prairie du Chien, Wis	602	Lake Superior	600
La Crosse, Wis	632	Lake Huron	576
Prescott, Wis	677	Lake St. Clair	570
St. Paul. Minn	690	Lake Erie	565
St. Anthony, Minn	760	Lake Ontario	232

Railroad Route from Milwaukee to La Crosse,
Via MILWAUKEE AND ST. PAUL RAILROAD.

THIS favorite railroad route runs west from Milwaukee, through a fine section of country, to WATERTOWN, 44 miles; there connecting with the *Chicago and North-western Railway*, running north to Fond du Lac, and Green Bay, the latter being 155 miles north of Milwaukee.

A railroad extends westward from the *Watertown Junction*, to Sun Prairie, to near Madison, the capital of the State, while the main line extends north-west, through Columbus to PORTAGE CITY, there uniting with the line of the La Crosse and Milwaukee Railroad proper, running through Horicon, about half way from Milwaukee.

At *Portage City* the Fox River Canal is passed, which unites the waters of the Wisconsin river with Lake Michigan, by means of the Fox river Improvement, terminating at Green Bay.

The *Fox River Canal*, 1¼ miles in length, flows from the Wisconsin river, at Portage City, into Fox river, thus uniting the tributary waters of the Mississippi and St. Lawrence rivers. The fall of water in the canal is 7 feet, affording good hydraulic power for propelling mills, and other manufacturing purposes. The elevation of the water, at Portage City, Wis., is 773 feet above the ocean, being 195 feet above Lake Michigan, and 173 feet above the Mississippi, at the mouth of the Wisconsin river.

From Portage City, the Milwaukee and St. Paul Railway runs through *Kilbourn City*, 109 miles, where the Wisconsin river is passed toward Lisbon, 135 miles. Here is a fine section of country, which is soon followed by a barren section, being, for the most part, clothed with a small growth of trees, while the soil is light and sandy.

Near *Greenfield Station*, 157 miles from Milwaukee, and 38 miles from La Crosse, are encountered the dividing bluffs which separate the La Crosse Valley from the tributaries of the Wisconsin river. Here is a tunnel, 68 rods in length, through which the railroad track passes, and poor land continues until near SPARTA, 27 miles from the Mississippi, when the rich La Crosse valley is reached and followed, the railroad running through a fine section of country.

From Sparta it is proposed to run a railroad north-west to opposite Winona, Minn., a distance of about 60 miles, crossing Black river, which is a fine stream flowing into the Mississippi near La Crosse, and affording along its valley an abundance of pine timber.

The railroad terminates at NORTH LA CROSSE, 195 miles from Milwaukee, where are commodious freight houses and the steamboat landing. Passengers are carried to and from La Crosse, half a mile distant, in omnibuses, over a bridge which spans the La Crosse river, here a sluggish stream.

For a description of LA CROSSE, see page 43.

Climate of Wisconsin.

WISCONSIN, lying between 42° 30' and 47° north latitude, extending to the south shore of Lake Superior, being bounded on the east by Lake Michigan, and on the west by the Mississippi river, is geographically considered one of the most highly favored of the States. "Its latitude would indicate a rather cold climate. Meteorological observations have demonstrated, however, that the mere circumstance of latitude is an unsafe criterion by which to judge of temperatures, since, within a given zone, owing to peculiarities of position, and configuration of surface, it not unfrequently happens that the terms north and south lose all their significance as indices of the distribution of heat.

"Bounded by great lakes on the north and east, and exposed on the south and north-west to the warm, moist winds of tropical seas in summer, and to the cold, and dry winds of sub-Arctic regions in winter, the scientific climatologist might with certainty predict an extensive range of temperature for the year between the maximum and minimum of summer and winter, respectively, as also between the mean or average of one and the other of these extreme seasons. And the results of numerous actual observations, extending through a series of years, show that the causes named do really produce those anticipated contrasts and local peculiarities, and to a very remarkable extent modify the climate of the State.

"Beginning with *Spring*, the season of planting, and early vegetable growth, and one of the most interesting of all, is that which indicates a mean temperature of 45° Fahr., for the season embracing March, April, and May. Commencing at St. Paul, Minn., or Hudson, on the St. Croix Lake, it passes successively, in a south-east direction, to near Portage, north of Madison, and there by a rapid southern descent to Chicago, Ill.; thus showing that the mean temperature of spring is as high in the north-western part of this State, even as far north as Hudson, as it is in Chicago, in northern Illinois. This is a remarkable fact, and, when generally known, can not fail to correct the erroneous impressions which now prevail as to the agricultural capacity of the climate of north-western Wisconsin.

"The Isothermal Lines (lines passing through points whose *Summer* temperature is equal) are also worthy of special attention. It will be observed that the mean of 70° Fahr. (which is the average temperature of Southern New York, and of Northern Ohio, Indiana, and Illinois) when it reaches Chicago, in its western course, suddenly bends northward, entering Wisconsin at Beloit, in Rock county, passing through Madison, the capital of the State, and then bears north-westward to the county of St. Croix, whose western boundary it cuts near Prescott, situated at the mouth of the St. Croix river, and from thence strikes St. Paul, continuing northward toward Pembina, situated on the Red river of the North."

By a reference to I. A. LAPHAM's "*Climatic Map of Wisconsin*," the range of summer and winter temperatures is most ingeniously and singularly shown; the influence of the Great Lakes tending to elevate the mean temperature of winter, and depressing that of summer.

STEAMBOAT EXCURSION,

FROM DUBUQUE to ST. PAUL, Minn., GIVING A DESCRIPTION of the CITIES, and VILLAGES, and OBJECTS of INTEREST on the UPPER MISSISSIPPI RIVER.

On starting from Dubuque, by Steamer, the river here being about half-a-mile wide, you encounter low wooded islands, which are continually in sight from the deck or the fleet boat, which is alike calculated for the accommodation of passengers and for the carrying of freight.

The bluffs on either side of the stream, rising from 100 to 400 feet above the water, are also continually in sight, being separated from one to five miles asunder, with wooded sides, or prairie-like appearance of the interior. No language can describe the beauty and picturesque variety of these bluffs and islands, as seen under different effects of light and shade—the bright moonlight vying with the noon-day sun of this transparent region.

POTOSI, Wis., 15 miles, is a flourishing town in Grant county, lying near the mouth of a stream of the same name. It is situated in a narrow and picturesque valley or ravine, through which the water flows. The town is divided into three settlements or villages, namely, *Dublin, Lafayette,* and *Van Buren,* altogether, being the most important place in the county. Large quantities of lead are mined in this and the adjacent counties, and shipped at Potosi in steamboats. Here are congregated about 2,000 inhabitants.

BUENA VISTA, Iowa, 15 miles further, is a small village lying on the west side of the Mississippi.

CASSVILLE, Wis., 34 miles above Dubuque, is a flourishing village and steamboat landing, from which large quantities of lead and agricultural products are shipped. Population, about 1,000.

GUTTENBERG, Iowa, 44 miles above Dubuque, is a thriving village, situated on the west side of the Mississippi, in Clayton county. Lead mines are worked in this vicinity, producing large quantities of ore; while the agricultural products shipped from this place are annually increasing in quantity. Population, about 1,200.

CLAYTON, Iowa, 12 miles further, is another flourishing village on the west side of the river. A large quantity of the surplus produce of Clayton county is shipped by steamboats at this place. Lead mines are worked near Clayton with considerable success. Population, about 1,000.

CLAYTON COUNTY, Iowa, extends 30 or 40 miles along the west bank of the Mississippi, and contained, in 1865, 21,922 inhabitants, mostly being engaged in agricultural pursuits. There were produced the same year in the county 897,063 bushels of wheat, 934,881 bushels of corn, and 607,928 bushels of oats, besides large quantities of other agricultural products.

McGREGOR, Iowa, 67 miles above Dubuque, situated on the west side of the Mississippi river, is an incorporated city of growing importance. It lies nearly opposite Prairie du Chien, Wis., which is the western terminus of the *Milwaukee and Prairie du Chien Railway,* being in close connection with both Milwaukee and Chicago by railroad routes. It was long known as "McGregor's Landing," being the depot of a large grain and produce market of wide extent, the interior country being very fertile and rapidly increasing in wealth and population. Here are several hotels, two banks, lumber yards, planing mills, saw mills, and other manufacturing establishments. Population, in 1865, 1,900.

The *McGregor Western Railroad* extends north-westward to the State Line, there connecting with the Minnesota Central Railroad, which is being constructed northward to St. Paul. It will also extend westward to the rich coal region of the Des Moines valley.

Prairie du Chien, Wis., is an old and interesting town, situated on the east side of the Mississippi river, 4 miles north of the mouth of the Wisconsin river, which is here elevated 600 feet above the Gulf of Mexico, being 71 miles above Dubuque, and 292 miles below St. Paul. By railroad route it is 194 miles west of Milwaukee, and 229 miles north-west of Chicago. The site is a level prairie, one or two miles wide, inclosed on the east by rocky bluffs, which stretch along the Mississippi on both sides for hundreds of miles. It is the western terminus of the *Milwaukee and Prairie du Chien Railway,* which runs through Madison, the capital of the State of Wisconsin, 98 miles distant. It contains 6 churches, a bank, several public houses, stores, and store-houses. Population, in 1865, 3,556.

Prairie du Chien is connected with McGregor, Iowa, by means of a steam ferry; it is also a great place for transhipment to the Upper Mississippi, several lines of steamers stopping here daily on their upward and downward trips from St. Paul to Dubuque and St. Louis.

The Railroad route from Milwaukee to Prairie du Chien, passing through Madison, is fully described on page 37.

LYNXVILLE, Wis., 14 miles above Prairie du Chien, is a small settlement lying on the east side of the river.

LANSING, Iowa, situated on the west bank of the Mississippi river, in Alamakee county, near the northern border of the State, 100 miles north of Dubuque, is a flourishing place, being first settled in 1852. Here are several manufacturing establishments, a national bank, 8 churches, hotels, stores, and warehouses, it being a great depot for wheat and other produce. Pop., in 1865, 1,675.

DE SOTO, Wis., 36 miles above Prairie du Chien, is a small settlement on the east side of the river.

VICTORY, Wis., 10 miles further, is another small settlement. Here the river bottom is wide, and numerous islands are passed.

BAD AX CITY, Wis., 56 miles above Prairie du Chien, in Vernon county, is the name given to a small village situated a few miles above the mouth of Bad Ax river.

BROWNSVILLE, Houston co., Minn., is favorably situated on the west bank of the Mississippi, 12 miles below La Crosse, being surrounded by an agricultural district of country producing large crops of wheat and other farm products. This town was laid out in 1853, and is a commercial point of growing importance. Here are several stores, and store-houses for grain, from which are shipped large quantities of wheat. Population, 800. The river-bottom is here wide, with numerous islands, the water rising and falling at this point usually about 15 feet. The town stands above high-water mark, under a high and picturesque bluff, called Wild Cat Mountain, elevated 500 or 600 feet above the river.

The City of **La Crosse,** La Crosse co., Wis., is situated on the east side of the Mississippi river, 84 miles above Prairie du Chien, standing 630 feet above the Gulf of Mexico; 210 miles below St. Paul, and 195 miles from Milwaukee by railroad route. It is a flourishing place, containing about 6,000 inhabitants, a courthouse and jail, United States Land Office, 8 churches, 2 banks, 10 hotels, 80 stores, 12 warehouses, 2 elevators, 5 steam saw mills, 2 steam shingle mills, 1 engine shop and boiler shop, 4 founderies, 1 ship yard, thrashing machine factory, 1 reaper and plow factory, 2 fanning mill factories, 2 flouring mills, 1 woolen factory, and 4 printing offices, besides many other kinds of mechanics' shops. The town is beautifully laid out in squares, and shade trees, consisting of elm, maple, and locust, adorn the streets. It is favored with a large amount of trade from southern Minnesota and the surrounding country, embracing the valleys of Black and La Crosse rivers.

Steamers land and receive passengers several times daily on their upward and downward trips during the season of navigation.

RUNNING the MISSISSIPPI RIVER by MOONLIGHT.

This magnificent stream above Dubuque presents varied beauties of the most romantic and picturesque character. As seen by moonlight from the deck of the steamer, during the summer or autumn months, nothing can exceed the panoramic view of its banks, reflected in the water below. If to this sublime effect be added the aurora borealis, or northern lights, when the sky is partially obscured by clouds, you have the most gorgeous reflection in the waters that can be imagined—the dark somber appearance of the forest being enlivened by the silvery color of the water, reflecting the moon and all the prominent stars in its bosom.

This effect is often witnessed for hours, when, if the clouds are dispersed, a fog often rises that effectually obscures the banks and the heavens above; then the bell is sounded, and the impatient steamer is run for the nearest shore, bow foremost, and made fast to a tree until such time as the fog disappears, which usually is soon after the sun rises on the ensuing morning.

The sun effect during the day, if clear, is equally magnificent when passing the castellated bluffs which line both shores for many miles above La Crosse, the water below reflecting in splendor all the colors and inequalities of the elevated headlands, as well as the rich forest trees that line its banks.

The numerous low islands, also, mostly wooded, are lovely in the extreme, often presenting a labyrinth that seems exceedingly intricate to all but the practiced pilot, who, from his eyrie in the wheelhouse, directs the motions of the steamer as if she were a thing of life. It is utterly impossible for pen or brush to describe the varied beauties of the Upper Mississippi—nothing but a visit to its romantic valley, from one to ten miles in width, with rocky bluffs, partly clothed with green verdure, can convey any idea of its pure dark waters, green banks, and the blue sky here witnessed during most of the season of navigation.

The villages and settlements that lie nestled along its shores at intervals of some ten or twelve miles, inhabited by an intelligent class of people, giving life to the scene, altogether stamps this noble stream as exceeding all others on the continent of America, if not in the wide world.

LA CRESCENT, Minn., lying nearly opposite La Crosse, is a steamboat landing. The village is situated on high table-land, about half a mile from the river. Here are 2 churches, 3 public houses, and several stores and store-houses. Population, 500. It is in contemplation to construct a railroad from this place to Winona, 40 miles, running along the west bank of the Mississippi.

RICHMOND, Minn., 18 miles above La Crosse, is a small settlement in Winona county, where the steamers usually stop to receive passengers and freight.

TREMPELEAU, Wis., 23 miles above La Crosse, situated in Trempeleau county, near the mouth of a river of the same name, is a flourishing village, surrounded by a rich agricultural country, producing large crops of wheat and other agricultural products. Here are several stores and store-houses, and about 1,000 inhabitants. The river-bottom is wide at this point, with several large islands along the Wisconsin shore, while the bluffs are truly grand and beautiful.

The City of **Winona,** Minn., the county seat of Winona county, is favorably situated upon a beautiful level prairie on the west bank of the Mississippi river, 195 miles above Dubuque, and 168 miles below St. Paul. It is surrounded by a fertile, well-cultivated, and populous section of country, being connected with the Wisconsin side by a steam ferry. It is the western terminus of the *Winona and St. Peter Railroad*, completed and in running order as far west as Rochester, 50 miles, and is being rapidly constructed west of that point to the Minnesota river.

The first white settlement was made in this place during the fall of 1851. In 1857 a charter was granted, and it was then regularly organized as a city. Population, in 1860, 2,468; in 1865, 4,439. Besides the city and county buildings, there is situated the Minnesota State Normal School, now in a very prosperous condition, 12 churches, 3 banks, 1 steam grist mill, 2 steam saw mills, 2 machine shops, 1 foundery, and several factories of agricultural implements, furniture, &c. Its hotel accommodations are good, there being several well-kept houses.

It is by far the largest wheat market in the State, and not second to any west of the Mississippi river. The receipt of wheat in 1860 was 1,600,000 bushels, and each succeeding year has marked some increase in this respect, it being justly considered the entrepot of southern and western Minnesota. A Railroad is now in progress of construction to extend from St. Paul to Winona, running for the most part on the west side of the river.

Winona and St. Peter Railway,

Finished to KASSON, 65 miles.

STATIONS.	Miles.
Winona	0
Minnesota City	6
Warren	2—8
New Boston	6—14
Greenwood	6—20
Richland	5—25
St. Charles	3—28
Saratoga	2—30
Chatfield	8—38
Preston	2—40
ROCHESTER	10—50
Kasson	15—65
Mantorville	3—68
Rice Lake	16—84
OWATONNA	13—97
St. Peter	150

☞ Connecting with Steamers on the Minnesota river, when finished.

FOUNTAIN CITY, Wis., 12 miles above Winona, is a flourishing village, situated on the east side of the Mississippi, where are a convenient steamboat landing and several stores and store-houses. Population, 600.

The beauty of the river scenery increases as you proceed on the upward trip toward Lake Pepin. The bluffs often appear like castles, being 500 or 600 feet in height; their shadows, being reflected in the pure waters below, seem like enchantment to the beholder.

MOUNT VERNON, Minn., is a landing and small settlement in the north part of Winona county.

MINNEISKA, Minn., is situated on the west bank of the Mississippi, at the mouth of Whitewater river, 130 miles below St. Paul. Here are shipped annually about 400,000 bushels of wheat, besides oats, barley, wool, butter, &c. Population, about 500.

ALMA, Wis., is a small village situated near the mouth of Buffalo river. Large quantities of wheat are annually shipped from this landing.

WABASHA, Minn., 249 miles above Dubuque, and 114 miles below St. Paul, is the county seat of Wabasha county. It contains a court-house, 4 churches, an academy, 3 hotels, 20 stores, and several large warehouses for the storage of grain and shipping purposes. The wheat trade is very large at this point, as Wabasha is the shipping mart for several counties in Minnesota, and the fertile and wealthy valley of the Chippewa, in Wisconsin. It is one of the most promising of the young cities of the State, having a fine location near the foot of Lake Pepin.

REED'S LANDING, Minn., 4 miles above Wabasha, is situated opposite the mouth of the Chippewa river, and at the foot of Lake Pepin, 35 miles below Red Wing. It is a flourishing village, from which large quantities of wheat are transhipped. As the river both above and below Lake Pepin opens earlier in the spring than the lake, passengers destined for points above are conveyed by coaches to Red Wing, and there re-embark.

LAKE PEPIN, an expansion of the Mississippi river, lying 670 feet above the Gulf of Mexico, being about 30 miles in length and 3 miles wide, is a most lovely sheet of water, lying between the States of Minnesota and Wisconsin. Here may be seen abrupt headlands, bluffs, and picturesque prairie slopes of great beauty; added to which, the purity and healthy influence of the Lake and surrounding country render this vicinity one of the most inviting resorts on the waters of the Upper Mississippi.

The villages and landings on both shores are being annually visited by great numbers of seekers of health and pleasure, during warm weather, and the early fall months.

SCENERY ABOVE WINONA.

The Maiden's Rock—Lake Pepin.

(Copied from Harper's Magazine, July, 1853.)

THE MAIDEN'S ROCK.

"Toward noon we entered that grand expansion of the Mississippi, called LAKE PEPIN. Its width is from three to five miles, and its length about twenty-five. It is destitute of islands, and all along its shores are high bluffs of picturesque forms, crowned with shrubbery, and commingled with dense forests. The white man has not yet made his mark upon Lake Pepin and its surroundings; and there lay its calm water, and yonder uprose its mighty watch-towers in all their primal beauty and grandeur. High above all the rest loomed the bare front of the Maiden's Rock, grand in nature, and interesting in its romantic associations. It has a sad story to tell to each passer-by; and as each passer-by always repeats it, I will not be an exception, It is a true tale of Indian life, and will forever hallow the *Maiden's Rock*, or Lover's Leap.

"*Winona*, a beautiful girl of Wapasha's tribe, loved a young hunter and promised to become his bride. Her parents, like too many in Christian lands, were ambitious, and promised her to a distinguished young warrior, who had smitten manfully the hostile Chippewas. The maiden refused the hand of the brave, and clung to the fortunes of the hunter, who had been driven to the wilderness by menaces of death. The indignant father declared his determination to wed her to the warrior that very day. The family were encamped on Lake Pepin, in the shadow of the great rock. Starting like a frightened fawn at the cruel announcement, she swiftly climbed to the summit of the cliff, and there, with bitter words, reproached her friends for their cruelty to the hunter and her own heart. She then commenced singing her dirge. The relenting parents, seeing the peril of their child, besought her to come down, and take her hunter lover for a husband. But the maiden too well knew the treachery that was hidden in their promises, and, when her dirge was ended, she leaped from the lofty pinnacle, and fell among the rocks and shrubbery at its base, a martyr to true affection. Superstition invests that rock with a voice; and oftentimes, as the birch canoe glides near it at twilight, the dusky paddler fancies he hears the soft, low music of the dirge of Winona."

THE SUN RISING ON LAKE PEPIN.

During warm weather, when a calm state of the atmosphere prevails in this latitude, the waters and shores of Lake Pepin present a grand and beautiful appearance. The break of day is often announced by a golden sky in the east, fringing the horizon, gradually giving way to a silver tint as the rising sun makes its appearance. Then the beauty of the land and water is enhanced by a contrast of colors, the silvery tint being given to the water, like unto a mirror of vast proportions, reflecting the sun so as to dazzle the eye in its direct rays, while the yellow bluffs and the green foliage of the forest give a grandeur and beauty to the scene as witnessed from the deck of an ascending or descending steamer—the only perceptible motion of the air being caused by the speed of the steamer, while the lungs draw in this healthy and life-restoring influence, rendering the spirits buoyant and hopeful. A thin gossamer mist, or fog, sometimes rises in portions of the lake, giving another variety and interest to the scene, which when dispelled by the noon-day sun, an extended and lovely view is presented of unequaled splendor.

NORTH PEPIN, Wis., 6 miles above the foot of the lake, is a small village lying on the east shore. Here the scenery becomes grand and interesting.

Lake City, Minn., 270 miles above Dubuque, and 93 miles below St. Paul, has a most beautiful and commanding position, overlooking Lake Pepin, situated on a prairie that was, until a few years ago, a half-breed reservation. The city lies within an amphitheater of bluffs that shield it from the prairie above. The entire plain is nine miles long, of irregular width, embracing about 10,000 acres of rich land. The whole view is commanded by several points, one of the most conspicuous of which is a sharp, tall peak, called "Sugar Loaf." From these the magnificent expanse of water and plain, and bluffs, and rocks, is spread before the eye for a distance of fifteen or twenty miles in either direction, lit up, as it were, by the transparent atmosphere and bright sky of Minnesota.

Lake City contains six churches, two banks, four hotels, three steam saw mills, a machine shop and plow factory, several stores and store-houses. Population, in 1865, 1,411, being surrounded by a rich and populous section of country.

The first English or American visitor to the Upper Mississippi, Captain Jonathan Carver, in 1766, paints in lively terms his delight in beholding Lake Pepin, and the country below it on the river. "In many places pyramids of rocks appeared, resembling old ruinous towers, at others, amazing precipices; and what is very remarkable, whilst this scene presented itself on one side, the opposite side of the same mountain was covered with the finest herbage, which gradually ascended to the summit. From thence the most beautiful and extensive prospect that imagination can form opens to your view." On the plain occupied by Lake City, he then saw "great plenty of turkeys and partridges," and "the largest buffaloes of any in America."

MAIDEN ROCK, Wis., 6 miles above Lake City. Here is to be seen some of the most beautiful scenery, for which Lake Pepin is justly celebrated.

FRONTENAC, Minn., is a small settlement on the west side of Lake Pepin.

RED WING, Minn., situated at the head of Lake Pepin, 64 miles below St. Paul, is one of the most beautiful places on the Upper Mississippi, being surrounded in part by high and precipitous bluffs, rising from the water's edge, 350 feet in height, near the steamboat landing. It is the seat of justice for Goodhue county, being well situated for trade, having a good agricultural region back of it, which here finds an outlet; the quantity of grain annually shipped from this place being very large. Here are six churches, several public houses, and a number of stores, warehouses, and manufacturing establishments. Population, in 1865, 2,362.

PRESCOTT, Wis., 36 miles below St. Paul, situated at the mouth of the St. Croix river, is a place of growing importance. It contains three churches, a bank, several stores, a large steam saw mill, and other mills and factories. Population, in 1865, 1,061.

The RIVER ST. CROIX, an important and beautiful stream, rises in Douglass county, Wis., near the west end of Lake Superior, affording many fine water privileges. Its general course is south, forming, in part, the boundary between the States of Minnesota and Wisconsin, and falling into the Mississippi 36 miles below St. Paul. The whole length is about 200 miles, and it is 100 yards wide at its mouth. *St. Croix Lake*, an expansion of the river, is 36 miles long, and three or four miles wide; commencing about one mile from its mouth. Several falls occur in the St. Croix, about the middle of its course, where is to be seen some beautiful river scenery. Steamers run on this river from its mouth to *St. Croix Falls*, 54 miles.

HUDSON, Wis., 16 miles above Prescott, the county seat of St. Croix county, is a flourishing village, being surrounded by a fine agricultural section of country, producing wheat in great abundance.

STILLWATER, Minn., 5 miles farther, lying on the north bank of the river, is well situated for trade, and is the depot for the extensive lumbering interests of the St. Croix valley. Steamers of a large class run from the Mississippi up to this place. It is the capital of Washington county, and contains, besides the county buildings, several churches, hotels, stores, and manufacturing establishments. Population, in 1865, 2,145.

Steamboat Route

FROM PRESCOTT, WIS., TO ST. CROIX FALLS, 54 miles.

LANDINGS.	Miles.	LANDINGS.	Miles.
PRESCOTT, Wis.	0	ST. CROIX FALLS, Wis.	0
Hudson, Wis.	16	Osceola, Wis.	9
Stillwater, Minn.	5–21	Marine Mills, Minn.	9–18
Marine Mills, Minn.	15–36	Stillwater, Minn.	15–33
Osceola, Wis.	9–45	Hudson, Wis.	5–38
ST. CROIX FALLS, Wis.	9–54	PRESCOTT, Wis.	16–54

FROM PRESCOTT to ST. PAUL, 36 miles.

POINT DOUGLASS, Minn., 35 miles below St. Paul, is a small settlement lying opposite Prescott, at the mouth of the St. Croix river.

HASTINGS, Minn., 32 miles below St. Paul, the capital of Dakota county, is advantageously situated on the west bank of the Mississippi. It occupies a most beautiful site, rising by easy grades to the prairie, and appearing to excellent advantage from the river; as a commercial point, it possesses advantages scarcely equaled in the State, commanding the trade of an area of hundreds of miles of interior country, fertile and populous. As a grain depot, few places possess the advantages that Hastings does, and, to accommodate this growing trade, many large and imposing warehouses have been erected. Besides the county buildings, here are five churches, the Minnesota Central University, several large stores and store-houses, three steam saw mills, an elevator, and several manufacturing establishments. Population, in 1865, 2,850. A railroad is in progress of construction, to run from St. Paul, on the east side of the Mississippi, here to cross the river and continue south on the west side to Winona, about 130 miles by railroad route.

NINNINGER, Dakota county, Minn., is a small village situated on the Mississippi river, 5 miles above Hastings.

After leaving Hastings, on the upward trip, a few small places are passed, the river here inclining to the westward until *Pine Bend* is reached, then the stream resumes its northward course to the city of St. Paul, the termination of navigation for steamers of a large class.

The City of **St. Paul**, a port of entry, capital of Minnesota, and seat of justice of Ramsey county, is most advantageously situated on the left bank of the Mississippi, 2,080 miles from its mouth, and 10 miles by land below the Falls of St. Anthony; being elevated 690 feet above the Gulf of Mexico; in lat. 44° 52′ north, long. 93° 5′ west from Greenwich. It is situated on a bluff, 60 or 70 feet high, rising to 100 feet, and presents a grand view from the river. It is near the head of steamboat navigation on the Mississippi, 5 miles below the mouth of the Minnesota river, which enters from the west at *Fort Snelling*, the river here being about a quarter of a mile in width. No place on the continent of America has a more commanding position or healthy location than this most favored city. Steamers of a large class, during a good stage of water, can descend to New Orleans, 2,060 miles distant; above the Falls of St. Anthony navigation is afforded, for steamers of a small class, for about 150 miles, while the St. Peter's or Minnesota river affords about a like extent of navigation, flowing through a very fertile section of country.

Saint Paul is one of the oldest settlements in the State. Father Hennepin visited and speaks of its site (1680). Jonathan Carver made a treaty in 1766 with the Dakotas in Carver's Cave, which is still in existence under Dayton's Bluff, within the present limits of the city. The site of the city was known to the Dakotas from time immemorial as "*Im-min-i-jaska*," or "*White Rock*," from its high bluff of white sandstone, a prominent landmark.

The first actual settlement was made in 1838 (just after the Indian title to the land east of the Mississippi had been extinguished) by one Parrant, a Canadian, who built a cabin on Bench Street. In 1840, a little log chapel was built by Father Gaultier, a Catholic missionary, on the present site of "Catholic Block." The church, or mission was called "St. Paul's," which henceforth became the name of the settlement. From this date the village grew slowly until the organization of the Territory in 1849, and the location of the capital at St. Paul gave it a new impetus. That spring there were only thirty buildings of all kinds in the village, but at the close of the season St. Paul contained several

ST. PAUL—PROGRESS OF MINNESOTA.

hundred people. At the first session of the Territorial Legislature, in November, the "town of St. Paul" was incorporated, with an area of 290 acres. On March 4, 1854, the "City of St. Paul" was incorporated, with 2,400 acres in its boundaries, which was amended in 1858, to include 3,200 acres, its present area. It has a river front of almost four miles. Its growth in population for a few years was perhaps unsurpassed by any city in the Union. In 1838 it had only three inhabitants; in 1846, 10; in 1848, about 50 (white); in 1849, 400; 1850 (census), 1,112; 1854, 4,500; 1857, 9,973; 1860 (census), 10,277; 1865 (census), 15,107.

The State House is a brick edifice, standing on elevated ground, from which a good view is obtained of the city and surrounding country. There are sixteen church edifices in the city, many of them being valuable structures, four national banks, and several firms engaged in the banking business, several hotels, numerous stores and store-houses, and several manufacturing establishments. This place has long been celebrated for its *fur trade*, which annually amounts to several hundred thousands of dollars.

(*Extract from the St. Paul Press, June 30, 1866.*)

ARRIVAL OF RED RIVER TRADERS AT ST. PAUL.

"The past two or three days an immense amount of furs and buffalo robes have been received by Pembina carts, and also by rail, from the Hudson Bay region. We saw yesterday at the railroad depot nearly one thousand bales of buffalo robes, making a pile as high as a house. They are being rapidly shipped below. There are ten robes in each bundle, making nearly ten thousand robes in all, worth from $10 to $12 each.

These are but a portion of those on the way down, which are estimated at fifteen or twenty thousand.

"In addition to the buffalo robes, there have been about a hundred bundles of wolf-skins and other furs, many of them very valuable. In all, there will probably be $300,000 worth of furs received at St. Paul this season, fully up to the amount marketed here in previous years, and maintaining the rank of St. Paul as one of the largest fur markets in the world.

"About 150 Red river carts were yesterday loaded up with groceries, miscellaneous, and Hudson Bay Company's stores, preparatory to making the long trip back to their hunting grounds on the shores of Lake Winnepeg, the Saskatchewan and Red rivers. Business, consequently, was unusually lively among the wholesale dealers, and the streets were crowded with the unmistakable residents of the far north-west, whose peculiarities of feature and costume are as distinctive as if they belonged to another race."

The arrival and departure of steamers are numerous, during the season of navigation, there being daily lines from St. Louis, Dubuque, and La Crosse, besides steamers to the St. Croix river, and up the Minnesota river to Mankato, 148 miles.

Railroads are also being constructed to run from St. Paul in different directions, making it the center of an extensive system of railways, diverging toward Lake Superior on the north-east, the Red river of the north, westward to the Missouri river, and south toward La Crosse and Dubuque.

Progress of Minnesota in Population and Wealth.

The following Table shows the general increase of population and assessed property valuation in the State at large, from the date of its Territorial organization, and the superficial expansion of settlement as indicated by the number of counties assessed. The census enumerations of population are given for the years 1850, 1857, 1860, and 1865, the population for the remaining years being estimated from the popular vote:

TABLE SHOWING THE GROWTH OF THE STATE SINCE 1850.

Year.	No. assessed counties.	Val. of pers. and real estate.	Population.
1850	6	$806,447	6,077
1851	3	1,282,123	7,000
1852	8	1,715,835	10,000
1853	6	2,701,437	14,000
1854	13	3,508,518	32,000
1855	18	10,424,157	40,000
1856	24	24,394,395	100,000
1857	31	49,336,673	150,037
1858	37	41,846,778	156,000
1859	40	35,564,492	162,000
1860	41	36,753,408	172,022
1861	44	39,077,531	190,000
1862	..	29,832,719	200,000
1863	..	32,211,324	225,000
1864	..	41,222,264	....
1865	43	....	250,099

POPULATION OF ST. PAUL.

The following table will indicate the growth of population since 1850:

Year.	Population.	Year.	Population.
1850	840	1857	9,973
1852	1,800	1858	10,000
1853	2,500	1860	10,600
1854	4,500	1864	12,500
1856	8,500	1865	13,176

St. Paul to St. Cloud, Minnesota,
Via the St. Paul and Pacific Railroad Route.

STATIONS.	Miles.	STATIONS.	Miles.
St. Paul	0	**St. Cloud**	0
St. Anthony	10	Clear Water Sta.	11
Manomin	8–18	Big Lake	14–25
Anoka	10–28	Elk River	9–34
Itasca	7–35	Itasca	5–39
Elk River	5–40	Anoka	7–46
Big Lake	9–49	Manomin	10–56
Clear Water Sta.	14–63	St. Anthony	8–64
St. Cloud	11–74	**St. Paul**	10–74

Early History of St. Paul.

The history of what is now St. Paul divides itself into three distinct periods, marked by corresponding changes of names.

1. The period of Indian occupancy till 1838, when it was known as *Imnijaska*, or "White Rock."
2. The period of squatter settlement, from 1838 to 1849, when it was known by the Indians as "the place where they sell whisky," and by the whites as "*Pig's Eye*."
3. Since 1849, when it was selected as the Capital of the Territory of Minnesota by the name of *St. Paul*, which had been bestowed upon it two years before.

EARLY HISTORY OF ST. PAUL.

First White Man in St. Paul.— Louis Hennepin, whose name is immortally associated with the history of Minnesota as the first white man who ascended the Mississippi within its borders, and as the discoverer of the Falls of St. Anthony, was undoubtedly the first white man who ever set foot upon the site of St. Paul. On April 30th, 1680, over one hundred and eighty-four years ago, Hennepin, a captive in the hands of a war party of Dakotas on their way to Mille Lacs, "landed in a bay, five leagues below the Falls of St. Anthony," a description of which, with other circumstances, fixes the locality under Dayton's Bluff, at the mouth of Trout Brook—about three quarters of a mile below the Steamboat landing.

The First American in St. Paul.— Eighty-seven years have passed since the arrival of Hennepin. Perrot has built and abandoned a fort on Lake Pepin, and planted the arms of France in Minnesota. Le Seuer has explored the Minnesota and given it the name of his gallant friend, Capt. St. Pierre. The Dakotas have been driven from the northern lakes by the Chippewas, and Minnesota, by the treaty of Marseilles, has just passed from the dominion of France to the flag of England, when on one fine morning in November, 1766, a keen, practical Yankee, the forerunner of all the Yankees in this part of the world, stepped into St. Paul near where Hennepin had landed three generations before. It was Brother JONATHAN CARVER, fresh from Connecticut, come to trade—Carver, great progenitor of the land speculators of Minnesota, first and greatest of the race.

Carver's Cave.— Jonathan's landing was at the foot of Dayton's Bluff, and his account of the discovery made there is the first memorial which links St. Paul with the traditions of the Dakotas:—

"About thirteen miles below the Falls of St. Anthony * * is a remarkable cave, of amazing depth. The Indians term it Wakan teebe, that is, *the dwelling of the Gods.*

"The arch within is near fifteen feet high and about thirty broad; the bottom consists of clear sand. About thirty feet from the entrance begins a lake, the water of which is transparent, and extends to an unsearchable distance, for the darkness of the cave prevents all attempts to acquire a knowledge of it. * * * * I found in this cave many Indian hieroglyphics, which appeared very ancient, for they were so covered with moss that it was with difficulty I could trace them. They were cut in a rude manner upon the inside of the wall, which was composed of a stone so extremely soft that it might be easily penetrated with a knife. * * * At a little distance from this dreary cavern is the burying-place of several bands of Naudowessie [Dakota] Indians. Though these people have no fixed residence, being in tents, and seldom but a few months in one spot, yet they always bring the bones of their dead to this place, which they take the opportunity of doing when the *chiefs meet to hold their councils and to settle public affairs for the ensuing summer.*"

These ancient burial mounds still exist on Dayton's Bluff, and, a few years ago, Mr. Neill had one of them opened. In this, which was 218 feet in circumference and 18 feet high, he found the remains of skulls and teeth at the depth of three or four feet.

In 1807, Major Long was obliged to creep through the sandstone *débris* at its mouth on all fours. In 1837, Nicollet worked for two days to effect an entrance, and confirmed the accuracy of Carver's description.

"A Chippewa warrior made a long

harangue on the occasion, threw his knife into the lake as an offering to Wakan tibi." Indian pictographs still remain, gray with age, upon portions of the wall still standing.

After a voyage to what is now Anoka, and up the Minnesota river for 200 miles, Carver, on the 1st of May, 1767, returned to the "Great Cave," where he officiated as the first representative of the whites in the great Annual Legislative Session of the Dakota bands, and made the first speech ever delivered by a Yankee in St. Paul.

"At this season," says Carver, "these bands go annually to the Great Cave before mentioned *to hold a grand council with all the other bands, wherein they settle all their operations for the ensuing summer.*" Thus early was St. Paul the *Capital of Minnesota.*

Nothing could be more significant of the geographical centrality of St. Paul than this fact, that from immemorial time it had, at that date, been the political centre of the scattered bands of the Dakota nation.

THE FIRST LAND SPECULATOR IN ST. PAUL.—It was here, too, at this "Great Cave," *that the first conveyance of land* was made and the *first deed signed* in Minnesota. This was the instrument by which the heirs of Carver founded their title to Carver's tract, which contained St. Anthony, St. Paul, and a large part of Wisconsin. The document is curious, and runs in this wise:

"To Jonathan Carver, a chief under the most mighty and potent George the Third, King of the English and other nations,. the fame of whose warriors has reached our ears, has been now fully told us by our good *brother Jonathan*, aforesaid, whom we rejoice to have come among us and bring us good news from his country.

"We, the chiefs of the Naudowessies, who have hereunto set our seals, do, by these presents for ourselves and our heirs forever, in return for the aid and other good services done by the said Jonathan to ourselves and our allies, give, grant, and convey to him, the said Jonathan, and to his heirs and assigns forever, the whole of a certain tract of territory or land, bounded as follows, viz.: From the Falls of St. Anthony, running on the east side of the Mississippi, nearly south-east, as far as Lake Pepin where the Chippewa joins the Mississippi, and from thence eastward five days' travel, accounting twenty English miles per day, and from thence again to the Falls of St. Anthony. We do, for ourselves, heirs, and assigns forever give unto the said Jonathan, his heirs and assigns, with all the trees, rocks, and rivers therein, reserving the sole liberty of hunting and fishing on land not planted or improved by the said Jonathan, his heirs and assigns, to which we have affixed our respective seals, at the Great Cave, May 1st, 1767.

"[Signed]
"HAW-NO-PAW-A-TON.
"O-TOH-TON-GOOM-LISH-RAW."

It was here, too, nearly a century ago, that Carver anticipated that splendid scheme of commercial intercommunication whose realization in our day is to make St. Paul the focus of the internal commerce of the continent. With the Delphic *numen* of the cave upon him, he foresaw that in the fat soil and laughing waters of Minnesota the elements were ripening for the sustenance of future populations, who, he says, will be "able to convey their produce to the seaports with great facility. * * This might also in time be facilitated by canals or shorter cuts, and *a communication opened by water with New York, by way of the lakes.*"

Here, too, Carver conceived the project of a Northern Pacific route by the way of the Minnesota and Oregon rivers, which, he says, "would open a passage for conveying intelligence to China and the English settlements in the East Indies"—an idea which will doubtless be consummated in our day.

THE ORACLE OF THE CAVE DUMB.—After Carver robs the "Great Cave" of its mighty secret that has throbbed for ages at its heart, the "Dwelling of the gods" is henceforth shut to all the world.

Henceforth, for seventy years, the oracle is dumb, silent, stony, impenetrable as the Sphinx, its white face turned in speechless prophecy toward the terraced slopes which lay there before its closed mouth.

History rolled over "White Rock" and past it, but took no notice of it. The brave Pike goes past it in 1805, and ignores it. Long besieges the unutterable oracle in vain in 1807. Fort Snelling is established in 1819. Mendota becomes the depot of the fur trade. Events are clustering around it, but all look past it, till 1837, when the Dakotas were persuaded to cede their lands on the east side of the river to the United States, on account of the valuable pine lands and water power thereon. The treaty was ratified at Washington in 1838, and *Imnijaska* ceased to be Indian territory.

Drive from St. Paul to the Falls of St. Anthony, returning via Fort Snelling.

This excursion affords one of the most interesting drives in any part of the country. On leaving St. Paul, by private conveyance, you pass through Madison avenue to the open plains which skirt the city, and then follow the direct road to St. Anthony, 10 miles. One or two beautiful cascades are passed near the roadside, as you approach the great Falls.

The *State University*, another object of interest, situated east of the road, overlooking the Falls, is a flourishing institution of learning. The town of ST. ANTHONY, with its saw mills and factories, propelled by water power, extends for near a mile above and below the Falls. Here is a *Suspension Bridge* of fine proportions, spanning the stream above the cascade.

MINNEOPOLIS, a large and flourishing place, is situated on the west bank, surrounding the Falls, where are very extensive saw mills, grist mills, paper mills, and other factories, all being propelled by water-power, and all well worthy of a visit. Here is a good hotel, where visitors usually stop for refreshments.

On returning, the road runs along the west bank of the Mississippi for four miles, when the *Falls of Minne-ha-ha* are reached. This beautiful fall of water, made famous by poetry and romantic scenery, is almost beyond description, as seen at different seasons. It has a perpendicular fall of about 40 feet, and can be viewed from the rear, as the rocks recede so as to allow a passage from side to side under the fall of water. About half a mile below, this pure stream enters into the Mississippi.

FORT SNELLING, two or three miles farther, and six miles above St. Paul, is an old Government post, where are usually quartered more or less troops; at the present time (1865) there are two regiments. Standing at the junction of the Minnesota and Mississippi rivers, on elevated ground, it has a very picturesque appearance. Here is a rope ferry across the river, leading toward St. Paul, it being reached by a circuitous road running under the bluffs, affording highly romantic views. Here the *Minnesota Central Railroad* crosses the Minnesota river.

The next object of interest is a Cave, 2 miles above St. Paul, which will well repay a visit to its subterranean caverns, from whence issues a lovely sheet of pure water.

MENDOTA, Minn., is situated on the right bank of the Mississippi river, at the mouth of the Minnesota, 5 miles above St. Paul. This is one of the earliest settled places in the State, being formerly the headquarters of the American Fur Company. Here are two churches, an hotel, and several stores. Population, 600. The *Minnesota Central Railroad* and the *Minnesota Valley Railroad* form a junction at Mendota, both rivers being crossed by a drawbridge.

FORT SNELLING, 6 miles above St. Paul, is an important United States post and rendezvous, situated on a commanding eminence at the junction of the Minnesota and Mississippi rivers, 6 miles below the Falls of St. Anthony.

The MINNESOTA, or ST. PETER'S *River*, one of the largest streams that rises in the State, is navigable for Steamers, at most seasons of the year, from St. Paul to Mankato, 148 miles, passing St. Peter and other important towns on its banks. In good stages of water, small boats run to the mouth of the Yellow Medicine, 238 miles from its mouth. Beyond this, at a slight expense, it might be rendered navigable to Big Stone Lake, where a portage of about three miles in length separates it from the equally navigable waters of the Sioux Wood, which empties into the Red river of the North. The Red river gives over 300 miles of navigable water on the western boundary of the State, before entering into British America, above Lake Winnipeg.

SHAKOPEE, capital of Scott co., Minn., is a handsomely situated village on the south bank of the Minnesota river, 22 miles from St. Paul by railroad. It was named in honor of an old Indian chief (a Sioux) by that name, and when translated into English is simply the short word "Six." At this point an important Indian town was located, known to the early settlers as "Shakopee's village." In 1865 it contained 1,250 inhabitants, five churches, one bank, two public houses, and several stores. The surrounding country is fertile and thickly settled.

CHASKA, Carver co., Minn., 38 miles above St. Paul, by Steamer, is situated on the North bank of the Minnesota river, which is always navigable to this point. Population, in 1865, 610.

CARVER, capital of Carver co., Minn., is situated on the left bank of the Minnesota river, 42 miles above St. Paul by Steamer. It lies at the head of navigation during the low water season, and is surrounded by a rich agricultural region. Population, 500.

BELLE PLAINE, Minn., 48 miles from St. Paul by railroad, and 69 miles by Steamer, is pleasantly situated on the south side of the Minnesota river. Here are three churches, three hotels, one flouring mill, one saw mill, and several stores. Population, about 1,000. The

Minnesota Valley Railroad will run through this place, when completed.

HENDERSON, capital of Sibley co., Minn., is situated on the Minnesota river, 80 miles above St. Paul. Population, in 1865. 1,000.

LE SUEUR, capital of Le Sueur co., Minn., 90 miles above St. Paul, is situated on the south bank of the Minnesota river, in the midst of the best agricultural section of the State. Steamboats land at this place daily, from which are shipped large quantities of produce. The Minnesota Valley Railroad will run through this place. Population, in 1865, 500.

ST PETER, the county seat of Nicollet co., Minn., is advantageously situated on the Minnesota river, 85 miles from St. Paul, and 150 miles from Winona by railroad route. Here are five churches, three hotels, two banks, and a number of stores. Population, 1,500. The Winona and St. Peter Railway, when completed, will terminate at this place.

MANKATO, the county seat of Blue Earth co., Minn., is situated at the great bend of the Minnesota river, about 140 miles from its mouth. It is the head of navigation during the greater part of the season, and is one of the best commercial points in the State. This is the proposed center of several railroads, which, when completed, will be of great advantage to this whole region of country, which for a great part is extremely fertile, and rapidly filling up with an industrious and intelligent population. Besides the county buildings, here are four churches, four hotels, two flouring mills, two saw mills, and several stores and storehouses. Population, in 1865, 2,654.

NEW ULM, the county seat of Brown co., Minn., is a flourishing village on the Minnesota river, about 60 miles above Mankato. The town was laid out in 1856, and improved steadily until the Indian outbreak of 1862. On August 19th of that year it was attacked, and partly burned, many of the inhabitants being butchered by the savages. Since that period, the place has improved rapidly, and now contains a population of about 1,000, mostly Germans.

Buffalo Hunt in Minnesota.

Extract from a letter, dated, ST. PETER, MINN., *Aug.* 1, 1865:

"I have just returned from the Redwood Falls, seventy-nine miles west of this town, and can assure you the trip has given me a good knowledge of the western portion of Minnesota. At REDWOOD a young town is starting into existence, already containing two hundred and sixty inhabitants, most all from Massachusetts and New York. The falls are thirty feet perpendicular over a solid ledge of granite, and already a saw mill is cutting the logs into building materials. In a distance of five hundred and sixty yards, there is a fall of one hundred and two feet. The river is narrow, but the scenery is wild and romantic in the extreme. In the rear of the village, the broad prairies extend west, I know not how far, but am told a hundred miles or more.

"Within eighteen miles, straggling buffalo are seen, and forty miles brings the traveler to the herds; sometimes they come in droves below the village. It may be of interest to your sporting men and those who may wish to see Minnesota in all its glory, and have a good time generally, to tell you that a hunting party, to capture buffalo, is to leave St. Peter on the eleventh of September. All the camp equipage, ponies, and all things necessary, can be obtained here.

FALLS OF ST. ANTHONY.

ST. ANTHONY—MINNEOPOLIS.

MINNE-HA-HA.

"Here the Falls of Minne-ha-ha
Flash and gleam among the oak trees,
Laugh and leap into the valley."

The City of **St. Anthony,** situated 10 miles north of St. Paul, by railroad, is one of the most favored localities in the State. It was incorporated in 1855, and in 1865 contained 3,500 inhabitants. Here are nine churches, two banks, three hotels, several stores, and numerous manufacturing establishments, propelled by water power. The "St. Anthony Falls Water Power Company" is capable of sawing 40,000,000 feet of lumber annually. There are also three flouring mills, a paper mill, foundry and machine shop, two breweries, and other extensive manufacturing establishments. The University of the State of Minnesota is located here, on an eminence overlooking the falls and the two towns. An elegant suspension bridge, erected in 1855, 620 feet long, spanning the main branch of the river above the Falls, connects the city with Minneopolis. The *St. Paul and Pacific Railroad*, completed to a point 50 miles northward, now extends from St. Paul to Big Lake.

Minneopolis, Minn., the capital of Hennepin county, is delightfully situated on the west side of the Mississippi, at the Falls of St. Anthony, where is afforded one of the most magnificent water powers on the continent. Here are four extensive flouring mills, a woolen factory, a sash, door, and blind factory. The capacity of its saw-mills is 50,000,000 feet; there are nine gangs of saws with rotaries, and the usual proportion of lath and shingle mills. In addition to these are manufactured ploughs, wagons, furniture, churns, barrels, &c.; two foundries, and the immense machine shops and car factory of the Minnesota Central Railway Company.

The Minneopolis Water Power Company, and the St. Anthony Company, have combined properties of quantity and availability unsurpassed in the United States. The lineal frontage along which the power can be carried and applied at a trifling cost, so as to supply a mill with power in every hundred feet of its course, is over 15,000 feet. The value of such a power, as well as the amount of machinery it is destined to propel, as the vast and fertile region north and west of it becomes settled, can hardly be estimated.

Here is a perpendicular fall of about 18 feet, and a rapid descent of 46 feet, with in a distance of one mile.

Besides the county buildings, Minneopolis contains three national banks, eight churches, four hotels, numerous stores and store-houses, together with many fine private residences. Population, in 1865, 4,600.

The picturesque scenery in and around these two cities at the Falls, their topographical beauty, the fine hard roads leading in all directions, the charming lakes in the vicinity, the celebrated *Minne-ha-ha Falls*, being a few miles below Minneopolis on the Fort Snelling road, taken together with the dry, bracing atmosphere that distinguishes Minnesota from all other Western States, have contributed to draw crowds of pleasure-seekers, travelers, and invalids to this locality.

Two beautiful lakes, Harriet and Calhoun, lying within a half hour's drive, and Lake Minnetonka, 12 miles westward, are places of constant resort in summer. These lakes, and about thirty others in the country, abound with sunfish, bass, and pickerel, as also the woods and prairies with the usual varieties of game. The old *Fort Snelling*, and its reservation of 10,000 acres, is situated in this county, at the confluence of the Minnesota and Mississippi rivers. The Fort is now used as a rendezvous for troops and recruits. Although once abandoned by the Government, the prospect now is that it will be permanently retained for military purposes.

The railroads terminating at Minneopolis, and passing through St. Anthony, are the *Minnesota Central*, running south and connecting with all the roads west of the Mississippi as far as Clinton, in Iowa; the *Minnesota Valley road*, running towards Sioux City; the *St. Paul and Pacific Railroad*, running west and east.

St. Paul and Pacific Railroad Route.

Manomin, the capital of Manomin county, is a small village on the east bank of the Mississippi river, 17 miles north of St. Paul by railroad route.

Anoka, Minn., 25 miles north of St. Paul, by railroad, is the county-seat of Anoka county, being handsomely situated on the east bank of the Mississippi river, at the mouth of Mille Lac, Rum river lying on both sides of the latter stream. The surface of the country is here diversified, and the climate highly salubrious; the soil being well adapted to agriculture. The natural meadows are an important feature, and, taken in connection with other facilities which the place affords, make it particularly adapted to the raising of cattle and sheep. Here are three church edifices, two hotels, several stores, and about 1,000 inhabitants.

Itaska, Anoka County, Minn., is a small settlement on the east bank of the Mississippi river, 35 miles from St. Paul by railroad route.

Elk River, Minn., is the name of a village situated on a stream of the same name, half a mile east of the Mississippi river, distant 40 miles from St. Paul, by railroad route.

Big Lake, Minn., the county-seat of Sherburne county, 50 miles north of St. Paul by railroad route, is situated about two miles east of the Mississippi river, containing a population of 200 or 300.

St. Cloud, Minn., lying on the west side of the Mississippi river, at the foot of the Sauk Rapids, is the capital of Stearns county, 74 miles north of St. Paul by railroad route. This may be called the head of navigation for the river above the Falls of St. Anthony, being on the direct route from St. Paul to the

Red river settlement of the North. The St. Paul and Pacific Railroad runs to this place. A railroad is also proposed to run from St. Cloud to Superior City, 120 miles, which, when finished, will be of immense benefit to this whole section of country.

The village now contains about 1,200 inhabitants, and is fast increasing in wealth and importance. There are a fine court-house and jail, one bank, United States land office, five churches, three hotels, twelve stores, and two printing offices. Here is an immense water-power, created by the Sauk Rapids, having a descent in half a mile of about 15 feet.

From St. Cloud to the Red river is about 200 miles, the distance being about 200 more miles to *Fort Gary*, British America. A large trade is carried on by means of ox carts passing over the prairie, including the furs and other articles belonging to the Hudson Bay Company.

SAUK RAPIDS, Minn., lying on the east side of the Mississippi river, at the head of the rapids, two miles above St. Cloud, is the capital of Benton county. It contains about 500 inhabitants, two churches, one hotel, two stores, and manufacturing establishments.

The *Mississippi river*, above the Sauk Rapids, flows through a level country, interspersed with groves of timber of different kinds, having a width of about 100 yards to Crow Wing, 40 miles above. North of the latter place, pine timber of a large growth is found in abundance, the lumbering business being the principal source of profit.

WATAB, Benton county, Minn., 80 miles above St. Paul, lying on the east side of the Mississippi river, is a small post settlement, containing about 150 inhabitants This is the terminus of the first division of the St. Paul and Pacific Railroad, branch line.

LITTLE FALLS, Minn., 100 miles north of St. Paul, is the capital of Morrison county, where are a fine water-power and saw-mills, it being in the region of a good lumbering section of country.

CROW WING, Minn., is the capital of Crow Wing county, situated on the east bank of the Mississippi, 120 miles north of St. Paul. This is an important post, where is located the Government agency for the Chippewa Indians, and commands a considerable Indian trade. It is on the line of the *St. Paul and Pacific Railroad*, which there crosses the river and will extend in a north-westerly direction to Pembina, on Red river of the North.

Northern Minnesota.

The distance from ST. PAUL to CROW WING, Minn., is about 120 miles, the *Chippewa Agency* being seven miles above Crow Wing, on Crow Wing river, a stream larger than the Mississippi proper; it is the outlet of Otter Tail and other numerous lakes, some sixty miles westward. The Indian agent for the Chippewa, Pembina, and Pillager Indians resides at the above agency. The agent makes a yearly payment to the above Indians, usually leaving the agency about the first of October, travels west to Otter Tail Lake, thence north, over the old Red river trail, to Douglas, Polk county, Minn., situated on Red Lake river, emptying into the Red river of the North, about forty miles west. In this vicinity the payments are made.

OTTER TAIL LAKE and the surrounding chain of lakes are of the purest water, abounding in delicious fish of different kinds. The shores are pebbly, surrounded by hard-wood timber, the sugar maple tree here predominating, from which large quanties of maple sugar are annually manufactured. The soil is unusually rich, producing wild grass three or four feet in height. The principal game left is wild fowl of different kinds, among which may be named the prairie chicken, grouse, partridges, ducks, and wild geese. Deer, elk, bear, foxes, badgers, and other fur-bearing animals, heretofore numerous, are now sparse, being nearly exterminated by the Indians, who are expert huntsmen. The healthy influence of this section of the country is unrivaled, it being a luxury to breathe the pure air of this region.

In September, 1865, a resident of Milwaukee, Wis., who had been suffering from ill health, tending to consumption, started for St. Paul and journeyed toward Crow Wing, along the east side of the Mississippi river, arriving about the time of the leaving of the United States agent and his party for the interior, the weather being then cool and delightful. Joining said party, and participating in their fare, he made the journey to Otter Tail Lake, and thence to Red Lake river, on horseback, returning with said party.

During this trip of some four weeks, his health was almost entirely restored, being able to bear almost any amount of fatigue; camping out in the open air, hunting, and fishing as circumstances would permit.

This is the happy experience of hundreds of invalids who have the resolution to visit this health-restoring section of country, where fevers and consumption are almost entirely unknown. Even the winter months are endurable and healthy in this region, extending north to the British settlement near Lake Winnipeg, 50° north latitude.

Buffalo and other large game may be found west of Red river, affording wholesome food, while wheat and vegetables are raised in great abundance wherever settlements have been made.

Interesting to Consumptives.

WHO SHOULD GO TO MINNESOTA AND WHO SHOULD NOT.

Extract from a letter, dated, ST. PAUL, *Minn., Dec.* 24, 1865:

"It is not the object of your correspondent to court any argument upon the relative merits of a northern or southern climate for the cure of that fell destroyer of human life and happiness, consumption, but merely to give his experience as an invalid during a sojourn of several months in a country which is fast becoming one of the most popular resorts for invalids from all parts of the Union. Neither do I wish to be understood as claiming for Minnesota entire immunity from disease, nor that the climate is a sovereign remedy for all cases of consumption; but, from careful observation, I believe I am justified in asserting that there is no locality on this continent so exempt from 'all the ills that flesh is heir to' as this. The dryness of the atmosphere, the peculiar character of the soil, the almost total absence of fogs and moist winds, all contribute to render the climate one of unrivaled salubrity.

In its first stages, consumption appears to yield readily to the peculiar influence of the climate; and, even in the more advanced stages of the disease, the patient, by a continued residence in this country, finds permanent relief and comparative good health. I find that three classes of cases arrive in this country in search of relief: 1. Those slightly affected, who take time by the forelock, get well in a few months, and return to their homes perfectly cured. 2. Those more seriously affected, who never fully recover the use of their lungs, but by a permanent residence in Minnesota enjoy comparative good health. 3. Those who wait until it is too late, and arrive here only to linger a few weeks and die among strangers.

"It is to be regretted that the majority of the invalids who arrive here are not of the first class. Unfortunately, owing to the ignorance of physicians, the disease is seldom detected in its first stages; and it is not until a hemorrhage takes place, or tubercles commence to soften, that they see the necessity for the removal of the patient to a more salubrious climate.

"The second, or predominating class, are scattered all over the entire State, from the Iowa line to the shores of Lake Superior. Go where you will through Minnesota and you will meet persons, apparently in good health, who could not exist two years under the influence of the cold moist winds of the Atlantic States. Many of them arrive here quite low, but, with the help of a good constitution and the peculiar salubrity of the climate, they manage to rally and enjoy tolerably good health. In one or two instances which came under my observation, the patients had to be removed from the steamboat in a carriage, and several months elapsed before any visible improvement could be noted; but finally the patients commenced to mend, and the clear, bracing atmosphere of winter soon restored them to health. A few Sundays ago we buried one of the oldest residents of this city, who had been ill with consumption for fifteen years. He had been sick with the disease three years when he entered the State, and did not expect to live many months; but he rallied, and by a continued residence in the country managed to prolong his existence a dozen years. Some of the leaning business men of this city, men noted for their enterprise and success in life, belong to the second class, and, although to all appearance in the full possession of health, tell you that it would be impossible for them to exist East.

"Of the third class not much need be said. They never ought to come here, as the fatigue and excitement of the journey only tend to hasten death. Some die on their way up the river, some at the hotels and boarding-houses before they have been domiciled among us a fortnight, and others, feeling that death is inevitable, start for home before they have been a week in the country.

"A very intelligent gentleman from New York, whose acquaintance I made when I first arrived in St. Paul, estimated that about three out of every ten persons who came here afflicted with lung complaints recovered so as to be able to return to their homes, and that over fifty per cent. of the invalids were afforded permanent relief. My informant, who is an invalid himself, has spent three years in the State, and, although in the enjoyment of apparent good health, says he will never be able to live in his native place again. He has therefore sent East for his family, and intends going into business here.

"It would be a difficult task to arrive at anything like the approximate number of invalids in the State, for there are no statistics on the subject, but it is safe to estimate them by thousands. In the summer you find them scattered all over the State, amusing themselves by fishing and hunting. The attractions in this respect are superior to anything of the kind in the United States perhaps. The entire surface of the State is dotted with lakes, varying in circumference from one mile to one hundred, which abound in the largest and choicest kind of fish. Pickerel, weighing from twelve to fifteen pounds, bass, wall-eyed pike and trout in proportion are caught in large quantities in all the lakes and rivulets. Trolling on the lakes is especially recommended by the physicians as the most fitting exercise for invalids who are too reduced to follow the more fatiguing sport of gunning. In the fall of the year, which is certainly a delightful season, the woods abound with deer, partridges and quail, while the stubble fields furnish the Nimrod with all the prairie chickens he can carry in an ordinary sized wagon. Geese and ducks of the finest flavor frequent the lakes in immense flocks, and afford splendid sport. Occasionally you stumble upon a bear, but invalids are not very partial to Bruin as a general thing, and usually allow him to follow the bent of his inclination unmolested.

"The cost of living in this far off Western country is by no means as expensive as some would imagine. Board at the best hotels in St. Paul can be procured cheaper than at the East, and in the country towns one can live very comfortably for about five or six dollars a week. As winter sets in, the invalids all flock to the towns, where they can spend the season more agreeably than they can in the country. Such places as St. Paul, Minneopolis, St. Anthony, St. Cloud, Farrihault and Winona are crowded with them, and the citizens derive no little profit by the presence of such visitors. The pineries, which extend along the St. Croix river, and run as far north as Lake Superior, are much frequented by consumptives. A belief is prevalent here that the pine emits an odor which is peculiarly healing, and highly beneficial for invalids; hence it is no uncommon thing for small parties to take up their quarters in the wilderness, and spend the winter there with the numerous gangs of lumbermen engaged in felling trees and hauling logs to the banks of the neighboring creeks, with the view of floating them down the St. Croix in the spring. Those who have the strength and courage to endure this wild mode of life generally experience the most beneficial effects, and in the spring are enabled to return fat and hearty."

Railroads of Minnesota, 1866.

The following Table, based upon information obtained from sources that are deemed reliable, presents the condition of Railroads now in process of construction:

NAME.	Miles completed.	Est of Miles to be finished by Jan. 1, 1867.
Winona and St. Peter Railroad	66	100
Minnesota Central Railway	56	112
1st Div. St. Paul and Pacific—Main Line	—	40
1st Div. St. Paul and Pacific—Upper Miss. Branch	50	74
St. Paul and Pacific—Winona Branch	—	80
Minnesota Valley Railroad	42	48
Southern Minnesota Railroad	20	40
Lake Superior and Mississippi Railroad	—	80
Total	234	474

Geological Survey.

The State Geologist, in his late researches, has confirmed the hope that vast and rich beds of iron and copper ore would be found within the counties bordering on the northern shore of Lake Superior; and in the vicinity of Lake Vermilion, in St. Louis county, he has discovered veins of gold and silver-bearing quartz, that promise to be highly valuable and productive.

Steamboat Route.

FROM CHICAGO TO MACKINAC AND SAUT STE. MARIE.

Ports, &c.	Miles.	Ports, &c.	Miles.
CHICAGO, Ill.	0	Annapee, Wis.	11–205
Waukegan, Ill.	35	Bayley's Harbor, Wis.	35–240
Kenosha, Wis.	16–51	Death's Door, Wis.	20–260
Racine, Wis.	11–62	(To GREEN BAY, 80 miles.)	
MILWAUKEE, Wis.	23–85	Washington Harbor, Mich.	13–273
Port Washington, Wis.	25–110	Beaver Island, Mich.	74–347
Sheboygan, Wis.	25–135	Pt. Waugoshame, Mich.	30–377
Manitowoc, Wis.	30–165	MACKINAC, Mich.	23–400
Two Rivers, Wis.	7–172	De Tour Passage.	36–436
Kewaunee, Wis.	22–194	SAUT STE. MARIE, Mich.	56–492

ROUTE FROM CHICAGO TO MACKINAC AND SAUT STE. MARIE.

On starting from the steamboat wharf near the mouth of the Chicago River, the Marine Hospital and depot of the Illinois Central Railroad are passed on the right, while the Lake House and lumber-yards are seen on the left or north side of the stream. The government piers, long wooden structures, afford a good entrance to the harbor; a light-house has been constructed on the outer end of the north pier, to guide vessels to the port.

The basin completed by the Illinois Central Railroad to facilitate commerce is a substantial work, extending southward for nearly half a mile. It affords ample accommodation for loading and unloading vessels, and transferring the freight to and from the railroad cars.

The number of steamers, propellers, and sailing vessels annually arriving and departing from the harbor of Chicago is very great; the carrying trade being destined to increase in proportionate ratio with the population and wealth pouring into this favored section of the Union.

On reaching the green waters of Lake Michigan, the city of Chicago is seen stretching along the shore for four or five miles, presenting a fine appearance from the deck of the steamer. The entrance to the harbor at the bar is about 200 feet wide. The bar has from ten to twelve feet water, the lake being subject to about two feet rise and fall. The steamers bound for Milwaukee and the northern ports usually run along the west shore of the lake within sight of land, the banks rising from thirty to fifty feet above the water.

LAKE MICHIGAN is about seventy miles average width, and 340 miles in extent from Michigan City, Ind., on the south, to the Strait of Mackinac on the north; it presents a great expanse of water, now traversed by steamers and other vessels of a large class, running to the Saut Ste. Marie and Lake Superior; to Collingwood and Goderich, Can.; to Detroit, Mich.; to Cleveland, Ohio, and to Buffalo, N. Y. From Chicago to Buffalo the distance is about 1,000 miles by water; while from

Chicago to Superior City, at the head of Lake Superior, or Fond du Lac, the distance is about the same, thus affording two excursions of 1,000 miles each, over three of the great lakes or inland seas of America, in steamers of from 1,000 to 2,000 tons burden. During the summer and early autumn months the waters of this lake are comparatively calm, affording safe navigation. But late in the year, and during the winter and early spring months, the navigation of this and the other great lakes is very dangerous.

WAUKEGAN, Lake Co., Ill., 36 miles north of Chicago, is handsomely situated on elevated ground, gradually rising to 50 or 60 feet above the water. Here are two piers, a light-house, several large storehouses, and a neat and thriving town containing about 4,000 inhabitants, six churches, a bank, several well-kept hotels, thirty stores, and two steam-flouring mills.

KENOSHA, Wis., 52 miles from Chicago, is elevated 30 or 40 feet above the lake. Here are a small harbor, a light-house, storehouses, mills. etc. The town has a population of about 5,000 inhabitants, surrounded by a fine back country. Here is a good hotel, a bank, several churches, and a number of stores and manufacturing establishments doing a large amount of business. The *Kenosha and Rockford Railroad*, 73 miles, connects at the latter place with a railroad running to Madison, the capital of the State, and also to the Mississippi River.

The City of RACINE, Wis., 62 miles from Chicago and 23 miles south of Milwaukee, is built on an elevation some forty or fifty feet above the surface of the lake. It is a beautiful and flourishing place. Here are a light-house, piers, storehouses, etc., situated near the water, while the city contains some fine public buildings and private residences. The population is about 10,000, and is rapidly increasing. Racine is the second city in the State in commerce and population, and possesses a fine harbor. Here are located the county buildings, fourteen churches, several hotels, *Congress Hall* being the largest; elevators. warehouses, and numerous stores of different kinds.

The *Racine and Mississippi Railroad* extends from this place to the Mississippi River at Savanna, 142 miles. The Chicago and Milwaukee Railroad also runs through the town, near the Lake Shore.

MILWAUKEE HARBOR.

Milwaukee, "THE CREAM CITY," 86 miles from Chicago, by railroad and steamboat route, is handsomely situated on rising ground on both sides of the Milwaukee River, at its entrance into Lake Michigan. In front of the city is a bay or indentation of the lake, affording a good harbor, except in strong easterly gales. The harbor is now being improved, and will doubtless be rendered secure at all times of the season. The river affords an extensive water-power, capable of giving motion to machinery of almost any required amount. The city is built upon beautiful slopes, descending toward the river and lake. It has a United States Custom House and Post-Office building; a court house, city hall, a United States land-office, the University Institute, a college for females, three academies, three orphan asylums, forty-five churches, several well-kept hotels, the *Newhall House* and the *Walker House* being the most frequented; seven banks, six insurance companies, a Chamber of Commerce, elevators, extensive ranges of stores, and several large manufacturing establishments. The city is lighted with gas, and well supplied with good water. Its exports of lumber, agricultural produce, etc. are immense, giving profitable employment to a large number of steamers and other lake craft, running to different ports on the Upper Lakes, Detroit, Buffalo, etc. The growth of this city has been astonishing; twenty years since its site was a wilderness; now it contains over 55,000 inhabitants, and of a class inferior to no section of the Union for intelligence, sobriety, and industry.

The future of Milwaukee it is hard to predict; here are centring numerous railroads finished and in course of construction, extending south to Chicago, west to the Mississippi River, and north to Lake Superior, which, in connection with the Detroit and Milwaukee Railroad, terminating at Grand Haven, 85 miles distant by water, and the lines of steamers running to this port, will altogether give an impetus to this favored city, blessed with a good climate and soil, which the future alone can reveal.

During the past few years an unusual number of fine buildings have been erected, and the commerce of the port has amounted to $60,000,000. The bay of Milwaukee offers the best advantages for the construction of a harbor of refuge of any point on Lake Michigan. The city has expended over $100,000 in the construction of a harbor; this needs extension and completion, which will no doubt be effected.

The approach to Milwaukee harbor by water is very imposing, lying between two headlands covered with rich foliage, and dotted with residences indicating comfort and refinement not to be exceeded on the banks of the Hudson or any other body of water in the land. This city, no doubt, is destined to become the favored residence of opulent families, who are fond of congregating in favored localities.

THE GRANARIES OF MINNESOTA AND WISCONSIN.—The La Crosse *Democrat* speaks as follows of the great strides of agriculture in a region which ten years ago was a wilderness. It says:

"We begin to think that the granaries of Minnesota and Northwestern Wisconsin will never give out; there is no end to the amount, judging from the heavy loads the steamers continually land at the depot of the La Crosse and Milwaukee Railroad. Where does it all come from? is the frequent inquiry of people. We can hardly tell. It seems impossible that there can be much more left, yet steamboat men tell us that the grain is not near all hauled to the shipping points on the river. What will this country be ten years hence, at this rate? Imagine the amount of transportation that will become necessary to carry the produce of the upper country to market. It is hard to state what will be the amount of shipments of grain this season (1863), but it will be well into the millions."

RAILROADS RUNNING FROM MILWAUKEE.

Detroit and Milwaukee (Grand Haven to Detroit, 189 miles), connecting with steamers on Lake Michigan.

La Crosse and Milwaukee, 200 miles, connecting with steamers on the Upper Mississippi.

Milwaukee and Prairie du Chien, 192 miles, connecting with steamers on the Mississippi River.
Milwaukee and Horicon, 93 miles.
Milwaukee and Western, 71 miles.
Milwaukee and Chicago, 85 miles; also, the River and Lake Shore City Railway, running from the entrance of the harbor to different parts of the city.

PORT WASHINGTON, Ozaukee Co., Wis., 25 miles north of Milwaukee, is a flourishing place, and capital of the county. The village contains, besides the public buildings, several churches and hotels, twelve stores, three mills, an iron foundry, two breweries, and other manufactories. The population is about 2,500. Here is a good steamboat landing, from which large quantities of produce are annually shipped to Chicago and other lake ports.

SHEBOYGAN, Wis., 50 miles north of Milwaukee and 130 miles from Chicago, is a thriving place, containing about 5,000 inhabitants. Here are seven churches, several public-houses and stores, together with a light-house and piers; the harbor being improved by government works. Large quantities of lumber and agricultural products are shipped from this port. The country in the interior is fast settling with agriculturists, the soil and climate being good. A railroad nearly completed runs from this place to FOND DU LAC, 42 miles west, lying at the head of Lake Winnebago.

MANITOUWOC, Wis., 70 miles north of Milwaukee and 33 miles east from Green Bay, is an important shipping port. It contains about 3,500 inhabitants; five churches, several public-houses, twelve stores, besides several storehouses; three steam saw-mills, two ship-yards, light-house, and pier. Large quantities of lumber are annually shipped from this port. The harbor is being improved so as to afford a refuge for vessels during stormy weather.

"Manitouwoc is the most northern of the harbors of Lake Michigan improved by the United States government. It derives additional importance from the fact that, when completed, it will afford the first point of refuge from storms for shipping bound from any of the other great lakes to this, or to the most southern ports of Lake Michigan."

TWO RIVERS, Wis., seven miles north from Manitouwoc, is a new and thriving place at the entrance of the conjoined streams (from which the place takes its name) into Lake Michigan. Two piers are here erected, one on each side of the river; also a ship-yard, an extensive leather manufacturing company, chair and pail factory, and three steam saw-mills. The village contains about 2,000 inhabitants.

KEWAUNEE, Wis., 25 miles north of Two Rivers and 102 miles from Milwaukee, is a small shipping town, where are situated several saw-mills and lumber establishments. Green Bay is situated about 25 miles due west from this place.

AHNEEPEE, 12 miles north of Kewaunee, is a lumbering village, situated at the mouth of Ahneepee, containing about 1,000 inhabitants. The back country here assumes a wild appearance, the forest trees being mostly pine and hemlock.

GIBRALTAR, or BAILEY'S HARBOR, is a good natural port of refuge for sailing craft when overtaken by storms. Here is a settlement of some 400 or 500 inhabitants, mostly being engaged in fishing and lumbering.

PORT DES MORTS or DEATH'S DOOR, the entrance to Green Bay, is passed 20 miles north of Bailey's Harbor, *Detroit Island* lying to the northward.

POTTOWATOMEE, or WASHINGTON ISLAND, is a fine body of land attached to the State of Michigan; also, Rock Island, situated a short distance to the north. (*See route to Green Bay, &c.*).

TRIP THROUGH THE LAKES. 69

On leaving *Two Rivers*, the steamers passing through the Straits usually run for the Manitou Islands, Mich., a distance of about 100 miles. Soon after the last vestige of land sinks below the horizon on the west shore, the vision catches the dim outline of coast on the east or Michigan shore at *Point aux Bec Scies*, which is about 30 miles south of the Big Manitou Island. From this point, passing northward by *Sleeping Bear Point*, a singular shaped headland looms up to the view. It is said to resemble a sleeping bear. The east shore of Lake Michigan presents a succession of high sand-banks for many miles, while inland are numerous small bays and lakes.

LITTLE, or SOUTH MANITOU ISLAND, 260 miles from Chicago, and 110 miles from Mackinac, lies on the Michigan side of the lake, and is the first island encountered on proceeding northward from Chicago. It rises abruptly on the west shore 2 or 300 feet from the water's edge, sloping toward the east shore, on which is a light-house and a fine harbor. Here steamers stop for wood. BIG or NORTH MANITOU is nearly twice as large as the former island, and contains about 14,000 acres of land. Both islands are settled by a few families, whose principal occupation is fishing and cutting wood for the use of steamers and sailing vessels.

FOX ISLANDS, 50 miles north from South Manitou, consist of three small islands lying near the middle of Lake Michigan, which is here about 60 miles wide. On the west is the entrance to Green Bay, on the east is the entrance to Grand Traverse Bay, and immediately to the north is the entrance to Little Traverse Bay.

GREAT and LITTLE BEAVER Islands lying about midway between the Manitou Islands and Mackinac, are large and fertile bodies of land, formerly occupied by Mormons, who had here their most eastern settlement.

GARDEN and HOG Islands are next passed before reaching the Strait of Mackinac, which, opposite Old Fort Mackinac, is about six miles in width. The site of Old Fort Mackinac is on the south main or Michigan shore, directly opposite Point Ste. Ignace, on the north main shore. *St. Helena Island* lies at the entrance of the strait from the south, distant about fifteen miles from Mackinac.

OLD FORT MACKINAC,* now called *Mackinac City*, is an important and interesting location; it was formerly fortified and garrisoned for the protection of the strait and this section of country, when inhabited almost exclusively by various tribes of Indians. This place can be easily reached by sail-boat from the island of Mackinac.

PTE. LE GROS CAP, lying to the west of old Fort Mackinac, is a picturesque headland well worthy of a visit.

The STRAIT OF MACKINAC is from five to twenty miles in width, and extends east and west about forty miles, embosoming several important islands besides Mackinac Island, the largest being BOIS BLANC ISLAND, lying near the head of Lake Huron. Between this island and the main north shore the steamer GARDEN CITY was wrecked, May 16, 1854; her upper works were still visible from the deck of the passing steamer in the fall of the same year.

GROSSE ILE ST. MARTIN and ILE ST. Martin lie within the waters of the strait, eight or ten miles north of the island of Mackinac, In the neighborhood of these different islands are the favorite fishing-grounds both of the Indian and the "pale face."

Mackinac, the Town and Fortress, is most beautifully situated on the east shore of the island, and extends for a distance of about one mile along the water's edge, and has a fine harbor protected by a

---

* Settled by the French under Father Marquette in 1670.

water battery. This important island and fortress is situated in N. lat. 45° 54', W. lon. 84° 30' from Greenwich, being seven degrees thirty minutes west from Washington. It is 350 miles north from Chicago, 100 miles south of Saut Ste. Marie by the steamboat route, and about 300 miles northwest from Detroit. *Fort Mackinac*, garrisoned by U. States troops, stands on elevated ground, about 200 feet above the water, overlooking the picturesque town and harbor below. In the rear, about half a mile distant stand the ruins of old *Fort Holmes*, situated on the highest point of land, at an elevation of 320 feet above the water, affording an extensive view.

The town contains two churches, five hotels, ten or twelve stores, 100 dwelling-houses, and about 700 inhabitants. The climate is remarkably healthy and delightful during the summer months, when this favored retreat is usually thronged with visitors from different parts of the Union, while the Indian warriors, their squaws and their children, are seen lingering around this their favorite island and fishing-ground.

The Island of MACKINAC, lying in the Strait of Mackinac, is about three miles long and two miles wide. It contains many deeply interesting points of attraction in addition to the village and fortress; the principal natural curiosities are known as the Arched Rock, Sugar Loaf, Lover's Leap, Devil's Kitchen, Robinson's Folly, and other objects of interest well worthy the attention of the tourist. The *Mission House* and *Island House* are the principal hotels, while there are several other good public-houses for the accommodation of visitors.

ISLAND OF MACKINAC.—The view given represents the Island, approaching from the eastward. "A cliff of limestone, white and weather-beaten, with a narrow alluvial plain skirting its base, is the first thing which commands attention;" but, on nearing the harbor, the village (2), with its many picturesque dwellings, and the fortress (3), perched near the summit of the Island, are gazed at with wonder and delight. The promontory on the left is called the "Lover's Leap" (1), skirted by a pebbly beach, extending to the village. On the right is seen a bold rocky precipice, called "*Robinson's Folly*" (5), while in the same direction is a singular peak of nature called the "*Sugar Loaf*." Still farther onward, the "*Arched Rock*," and other interesting sights, meet the eye of the explorer, affording pleasure and delight, particularly to the scientific traveller and lover of nature. On the highest ground, elevated 320 feet above the waters of the Strait, is the signal station (4), situated near the ruins of old *Fort Holmes*.

The settlement of this Island was commenced in 1764. In 1793 it was surrendered to the American government; taken by the British in 1812; but restored by the treaty of Ghent, signed in Nov., 1814

The Lover's Leap.—Mackinac Island.

The huge rock called the "Lover's Leap," is situated about one mile west of the village of Mackinac. It is a high perpendicular bluff, 150 to 200 feet in height, rising boldly from the shore of the Lake. A solitary pine-tree formerly stood upon its brow, which some Vandal has cut down.

Long before the pale faces profaned this island home of the Genii, Me-che-ne-mock-e-nung-o-qua, a young Ojibway girl, just maturing into womanhood, often wandered there, and gazed from its dizzy heights and witnessed the receding canoes of the large war parties of the combined bands of the Ojibways and Ottawas, speeding South, seeking for fame and scalps.

It was there she often sat, mused, and hummed the songs Ge-niw-e-gwon loved; this spot was endeared to her, for it was there that she and Ge-niw-e-gwon first met and exchanged words of love, and found an affinity of souls or spirits existing between them. It was there she often sat and sang the Ojibway love song—

"Mong-e-do-gwain, in-de-nain-dum,
Mong-e-do-gwaip, in-de-nain-dum;
Wain-shung-ish-ween, neen-e-mo-shane,
Wain-shung-ish-ween, neen-e-mo-shane,
A-nee-wau-wau-sau-bo-a-zode,
A-nee-wau-wau-sau-bo-a-zode."

I give but one verse, which may be translated as follows:

A loon, I thought was looming,
A loon, I thought was looming;
Why! it is he, my lover,
Why! it is he, my lover.
His paddle, in the waters gleaming,
His paddle in the waters gleaming.

From this bluff she often watched and listened for the return of the war parties, for amongst them she knew was Ge-niw-e-gwon; his head decorated with war-eagle plumes, which none but a brave could sport. The west wind often wafted far in advance the shouts of victory and death, as they shouted and sang upon leaving Pe-quot-e-nong (old Mackinac), to make the traverse to the Spirit, or Fairie Island.

One season, when the war party returned, she could not distinguish his familiar and loved war-shout. Her thinking spirit, or soul (presentiment) told her that he had gone to the Spirit Land of the west. It was so, an enemy's arrow had pierced his breast, and after his body was placed leaning against a tree, his face fronting his enemies he died; but ere he died he wished the mourning warriors to remember him to the sweet maid of his heart. Thus he died far away from home and the friends he loved.

Me-che-ne-mock-e-nung-o-qua's heart hushed its beatings, and all the warm emotions of that heart were chilled and dead. The moving, living spirit or soul of her beloved Ge-niw-e-gwon she witnessed, continually beckoning her to follow him to the happy hunting grounds of spirits in the west—he appeared to her in human shape, but was invisible to others of his tribe.

One morning her body was found mangled at the foot of the bluff. The soul had thrown aside its covering of earth, and had gone to join the spirit of her beloved Ge-niw-e-gwon, to travel together to the land of spirits, realizing the glories and bliss of a future, eternal existence.

Yours, &c.,
Wm. M. J * * * * * *

ALTITUDE OF VARIOUS POINTS ON ISLAND OF MACKINAC.

Localities.	Above Lake Huron.	Above the Sea.
Lake Huron	000 feet.	574 feet.
Fort Mackinac	150 "	724 "
Old Fort Holmes	315 "	889 "
Robinson's Folly	128 "	702 "
Chimney Rock	131 "	705 "
Top of Arched Rock	140 "	714 "
Lover's Leap	145 "	719 "
Summit of Sugar Loaf	284 "	858 "
Principal Plateau of Mackinac Island	160 "	734 "
Upper Plateau	300 "	874 "
La Cloche Mountain, north side Lake Huron, C. W.	1,200 "	1,774 "

The whole Island of Mackinac is deeply interesting to the scientific explorer, as well as to the seeker of health and pleasure. The following extract, illustrated by an engraving, is copied from "FOSTER and WHITNEY'S *Geological Report*" of that region:

"As particular examples of denuding action on the island, we would mention the 'Arched Rock' and the 'Sugar Loaf.' The former, situated on the eastern shore, is a feature of great interest. The cliffs here attain a height of nearly one hundred feet, while at the base are strewn numerous fragments which have fallen from above. The *Arched Rock* has been excavated in a projecting angle of the limestone cliff, and the top of the span is about ninety feet above the lake-level, surmounted by about ten feet of rock. At the base of a projecting angle, which rises up like a buttress, there is a small opening, through which an explorer may pass to the main arch, where, after clambering over the steep slope of debris and the projecting edges of the strata, he reaches the brow of the cliff.

"The beds forming the summit of the arch are cut off from direct connection with the main rock by a narrow gorge of no great depth. The portion supporting the arch on the north side, and the curve of the arch itself, are comparatively fragile, and cannot, for a long period, resist the action of rains and frosts, which, in this latitude, and on a rock thus constituted, produce great ravages every season. The arch, which on one side now connects this abutment with the main cliff, will soon be destroyed, as well as the abutment itself, and the whole be precipitated into the lake.

"It is evident that the denuding action roducing such an opening, with other attendant phenomena, could only have operated while near the level of a large body of water like the great lake itself; and we find a striking similarity between the denuding action of the water here in time past, and the same action as now manifested in the range of the *Pictured Rocks* on the shores of Lake Superior. As an interesting point in the scenery of this island, the Arched Rock attracts much attention, and in every respect is worthy of examination." (*See Engraving*.)

Other picturesque objects of great interest, besides those enumerated above, occur at every turn on roving about this enchanting island, where the pure, bracing air and clear waters afford a pleasurable sensation, difficult to be described unless visited and enjoyed.

The bathing in the pure waters of the Strait at this place is truly delightful, affording health and vigor to the human frame.

The Island of Mackinac.

ROMANTIC AND PICTURESQUE APPEARANCE OF THE ISLAND AND SURROUNDING COUNTRY—ITS PURITY OF ATMOSPHERE —A MOONLIGHT EXCURSION, &c., &c.

—— " From whose rocky turrets battled high,
Prospect immense spread out on all sides round;
Lost now between the welkin and the main,
Now walled with hills that slept above the storm,
Most fits such a place for musing men;
Happiest, sometimes, when musing without aim."
[POLLOK.

In this Northern region, Nature has at last fully resumed her green dress. Flowers wild, but still beautiful, bloom and disappear in succession. Birds of various hues have returned to our groves, and welcome us as we trace these shady walks. "In all my wand'rings round this world of care," I have found no place wherein the climate, throughout the summer season, seems to exercise on the human constitution a more beneficial influence than on this Island. In other parts of this country and in Europe, the places of *Resort* are beautiful, indeed; but a certain oppressiveness there at times pervades the air, that a person even with the best health in the world, feels a lassitude creeping through his frame. Here, we seldom, if ever, experience such a feeling from this cause. For the western breeze even in the hottest days passing over this island, keeps the air cool, and, especially if proper exercise be taken by walking or riding, one feels a bracing up, a certain buoyancy of spirits that is truly astonishing.

Ye inhabitants of warm latitudes, who pant in cities for a breath of cool air, fly to this isle for comfort. Ye invalid, this is the place in which to renovate your shattered constitution. The lovers of beautiful scenery or the curious in nature, and the artist, whose magic pencil delights to trace nature's lineaments, need not sigh for the sunny clime of Italy for subjects on which to feed the taste and imagination.

This island is intersected by fine carriage roads, shaded here and there by a young growth of beech, maple, and other trees. On the highest part of it, about 300 feet, are the ruins of Old Fort Holmes. From this point of elevation, the scenery around is extensive and beautiful. In sight, are some localities connected with "the tales of the times of old," both of the savage and the civilized. Looking westwardly, and at the distance of about four miles across an arm of Lake Huron, is Point St. Ignace, which is the southernmost point of land, of the greater portion of the Upper Peninsula. Immediately south of it are the "Straits of Mackinac," which separating the Northern and Southern Peninsulas from each other, are about four miles wide. On the south shore, may still be seen traces of Old Fort Mackinac, which is well known in history as having been destroyed by Indians, in 1763, at the instigation of Pontiac, an Indian Chief. Turning our gaze southeastwardly, we see the picturesque "Round Island," as it were at our feet. And further on, is "Bois-Blanc Island," stretching away with its winding shores, far into Lake Huron. Look to the east, and there stands this inland sea, apparently "boundless and deep," and "pure as th' expanse of heaven." Directly north from our place of observation, are the "Islands of St. Martin;" while beyond them in the Bay, are two large rivers—the Pine, and Carp Rivers. And lastly, casting our eyes towards the northwest, we see on the main land the two "Sitting Rabbits;" being two singular looking hills or rocks, and so called by the Indians from some resemblance at a distance to rabbits in a sitting posture. As a whole, this scenery presents, hills, points of land jutting into the lake, and "straits," bays, and islands. Here, the lake contracts itself into narrow channels, or straits, which at times are whitened by numerous sails of commerce; and there, it spreads itself away as far as the eye can reach. And, while contemplating this scene, perhaps a dark column of smoke, like the Genii in the Arabian Tales, may be seen rising slowly out of the bosom of Lake Huron, announcing the approach of the Genii of modern days, the Steamboat! Let us descend to the shore.

It is evening! The sun, with all his glory has disappeared in the west; but the moon sits in turn the arbitress of heaven. And now—

"How sweet the moonlight sleeps upon this bank;
Here will we sit, and let the sounds of music
Creep in our ears; soft stillness and the night,
Becomes the touches of sweet harmony."

Such a moonlight night I once enjoyed. The hum of day-life had gradually subsided, and there was naught to disturb the stillness of the hour, save the occasional laughter of those who lingered out in the open air. In the direction of the moon, and on the Lake before me, there was a broad road of light trembling upon its bosom. A few moments more, two small boats with sails up to catch the gentle breeze, were seen passing and re-passing this broad road of light. Then the vocal song was raised on the waters, and woman's voice was borne on moonlight beam to the listening ear in the remotest shades. The voices became clearer and stronger as the boats approached nearer; then, again, dying away in the distance, seemed to be merged with the mellow rays of the moon. But let us leave poetry and fancy aside, and come to matters of fact, matters of accommodation, prepared for those who may favor our island with their visits this summer.

There are several large hotels, with attentive hosts, ever ready to contribute towards the comforts of their visitors. Walking, riding, fishing, shooting, and sailing can be here pursued with great benefit to health. We have billiard-rooms and bowling-alleys; in the stores are found Indian curiosities; and, perhaps, the Indians themselves, who resort to this island on business, may be curiosities to those who have never seen them; they are the true "native Americans," the *citizens* of this North American Republic.

ROUND ISLAND is a small body of land lying a short distance southeast of Mackinac, while BOIS BLANC ISLAND is a large body of land lying still farther in the distance, in the Straits of Mackinac.

ST. MARTIN'S BAY, and the waters contiguous, lying north of Mackinac, afford fine fishing grounds, and are much resorted to by visitors fond of aquatic sports. *Great St. Martin's* and *Little St. Martin's Islands* are passed before entering the bay, and present a beautiful appearance.

CARP and PINE rivers are two small streams entering into St. Martin's Bay, affording an abundance of brook trout of a large size. From the head of the above bay to the foot of Lake Superior, is only about 30 miles in a northerly direction, passing through a wilderness section of country, sparsely inhabited by Indians, who have long made this region their favored hunting and fishing grounds.

POINT DE TOUR, 36 miles east from Mackinac, is the site of a light-house and settlement, at the entrance of St. Mary's River, which is here about half a mile in width; this passage is also called the West Channel. At a distance of about two miles above the Point is a new settlement, where have been erected a steamboat pier, a hotel, and several dwellings.

DRUMMOND ISLAND, a large and important body of land belonging to the United States, is passed on the right, where are to be seen the ruins of an old fort erected by the British. On the left is the mainland of Northern Michigan. Ascending St. Mary's River, next is passed ROUND or PIPE ISLAND, and other smaller islands on the right, presenting a beautiful appearance, most of them belonging to the United States.

ST. JOSEPH ISLAND, 10 miles above Point de Tour, is a large and fertile island belonging to Canada. It is about 20 miles long from east to west, and about 15 miles broad, covered in part with a heavy growth of forest-trees. Here are seen the ruins of an old fort erected by the British, on a point of land commanding the channel of the river.

CARLTONVILLE is a small settlement on the Michigan side of the river, 12 miles above the De Tour. Here is a steam saw-mill and a few dwelling-houses.

LIME ISLAND is a small body of land belonging to the United States, lying in the main channel of the river, about 12 miles from its mouth. The channel here forms the boundary between the United States and Canada.

MUD LAKE, as it is called, owing to its waters being easily riled, is an expansion of the river, about five miles wide and ten miles long, but not accurately delineated on any of the modern maps, which appear to be very deficient in regard to St. Mary's River and its many islands—presenting at several points most beautiful river scenery. In the St. Mary's River there are about fifty islands belonging to the United States, besides several attached to Canada.

NEBISH ISLAND, and *Sailor's Encampment*, situated about half way from the Point to the Saut, are passed on the left while sailing through the main channel.

SUGAR ISLAND, a large body of fertile land belonging to the United States, is reached about 30 miles above Point de Tour, situated near the head of St. Joseph Island. On the right is passed the *British* or *North Channel*, connecting on the east with Georgian Bay. Here are seen two small rocky islands belonging to the British Government, which command both channels of the river.

The *Nebish Rapids* are next passed by the ascending vessel, the stream here running about five knots per hour. The mainland of Canada is reached immediately above the rapids, being clothed with a dense growth of forest-trees of small size. To the north is a dreary wilderness, extending through to Hudson Bay, as yet almost wholly unexplored and unknown, except to the Indian or Canadian hunter.

LAKE GEORGE, twenty miles below the Saut, is another expansion of the river, being about five miles wide and eight miles long. Here the channel is only from eight to ten feet in depth for about one mile, forming a great impediment to navigation.*

CHURCH'S LANDING, on Sugar Island, twelve miles below the Saut, is a steamboat landing; opposite it is SQUIRREL ISLAND, belonging to the Canadians. This is a convenient landing, where are situated a store and dwelling. The industrious occupants are noted for the making of *raspberry jam*, which is sold in large quantities, and shipped to Eastern and Southern markets.

Garden River Settlement is an Indian village ten miles below the Saut, on the Canadian shore. Here are a missionary church and several dwellings, surrounded by grounds poorly cultivated, fishing and hunting being the main employment of the Chippewa Indians who inhabit this section of country. Both sides of the river abound in wild berries of good flavor, which are gathered in large quantities by the Indians, during the summer months.

Extract from a letter dated SAUT STE MARIE, Sept., 1854:

"The scenery of the St. Mary's River seems to grow more attractive every year. There is a delicious freshness in the countless evergreen islands that dot the river in every direction, from the Falls to Lake Huron, and I can imagine of no more tempting retreats from the dusty streets of towns, in summer, than these islands; I believe the time will soon come when neat summer cottages will be scattered along the steamboat route on these charming islands. A summer could be delightfully spent in exploring for new scenery and in fishing and sailing in these waters.

"And Mackinac, what an attractive little piece of *terra firma* is that island—half ancient, half modern! The view from the fort is one of the finest in the world. Perched on the brink of a precipice some two hundred feet above the bay—one takes in at a glance from its walls the harbor, with its numerous boats and the pretty village; and the whole rests on one's vision more like a picture than a reality. Every thing on the island is a curiosity; the roads or streets that wind around the harbor or among the grove-like forests of the island are naturally pebbled and macadamized; the buildings are of every style, from an Indian lodge to a fine English house. The island is covered with charming natural scenery, from the pretty to the grand, and one may spend weeks constantly finding new objects of interest and new scenes of beauty. It is unnecessary to particularize—every visitor will find

---

* A new channel has been formed, by dredging, which gives a greater depth of water.

them, and enjoy the sight more than any description.

"The steamers all call there, on their way to and from Chicago, and hundreds of small sail vessels, in the fishing trade, have here their head-quarters. Drawn upon the pebbled beach or gliding about the little bay are bark canoes and the far-famed 'Mackinac boats,' without number. These last are the perfection of light sail-boats, and I have often been astonished at seeing them far out in the lake, beating up against winds that were next to gales. Yesterday the harbor was thronged with sail boats and vessels of every description, among the rest were the only two iron steamers that the United States have upon all the lakes, the 'Michigan' and the 'Surveyor,' formerly called the 'Abert,' employed in the Coast Survey.

"For a wonder, Lake Huron was calm and at rest for its entire length, and the steamer 'Northerner' made a beautiful and quick passage from Mackinac to this place. The weather continues warm and dry, and hundreds are regretting they have so early left the Saut and Mackinac, and we believe you will see crowds of visitors yet. JAY."

St. Mary's River.

By a careful examination of the Government Charts of the Straits of Mackinac and River Ste. Marie, published in 1857, it appears that the *Point De Tour Light-House* is situated in 45° 57′ N. Lat., being 36 miles to the eastward of Fort Mackinac. The width of the De Tour passage is about one mile, with a depth of water of 100 feet and upwards, although but 50 feet is found off the light, as you run into Lake Huron. *Drummond Island*, attached to the United States, lies on the east, while the main shore of Michigan lies to the west of the entrance. *Pipe Island*, 4 miles, is first passed on ascending the stream, and then *Lime Island*, 6 miles further. *St. Joseph's Island*, with its old fort, attached to Canada, lies 8 miles from the entrance. *Potagannissing Bay*, dotted with numerous small islands, mostly belonging to the United States, is seen lying to the eastward, communicating with the North Channel. *Mud Lake*, 6 miles further, is next entered, having an expanse of about 4 miles in width, when *Sailor's Encampment Island* is reached, being 20 miles from Lake Huron. The head of St. Joseph's and part of *Sugar Island* are reached 26 miles northward from the De Tour, where diverges the Canadian or North Channel, running into the Georgian Bay; this channel is followed by the Canadian steamers. The *Nebish Rapids* are next passed, and *Lake George* entered, 6 miles further, being 32 miles from Lake Huron. This lake or expansion of the river is 9 miles in length and 4 miles broad, affording 12 feet of water over the shoals and terminating at *Church's Landing*, lying opposite *Squirrel Island*, attached to Canada. *Garden River Settlement*, 3 miles, is an Indian town on the Canada side. *Little Lake George* is passed and *Point Aux Pins* reached, 3 miles further. From Little

Lake George to the *Saut Ste. Marie*, passing around the head of Sugar Island, is 8 miles further; being 55 miles from Lake Huron. The *Rapids*, or *Ship Canal*, extend for about one mile, overcoming a fall of 20 feet, when a beautiful stretch of the river is next passed and *Waiska Bay* entered, 6 miles above the rapids; making the St. Mary's River 62 miles in length. The channel forming the boundary line between Canada and the United States is followed by the ascending steamer from the lower end of St. Joseph's Island to Lake Superior, while a more direct passage is afforded for vessels of light draught through *Hay Lake*, lying west of Sugar Island and entering Mud Lake. Nothing can be more charming than a trip over these waters, when sailing to or from the Straits of Mackinac, thus having in view rich and varied lake and river scenery, once the exclusive and favored abode of the red man of the forest, now fast passing away before the march of civilization.

Saut Ste. Marie,[*] capital of Chippewa Co., Mich., is advantageously situated on St. Mary's River, or Strait, 350 miles N.N.W. of Detroit, and 15 miles from the foot of Lake Superior, in N. lat. 46° 31'. The Rapids at this place, giving the name to the settlements on both sides of the river, have a descent of 20 feet within the distance of a mile, and form the natural limit of navigation. The Ship Canal, however, which has recently been constructed on the American side, obviates this difficulty. Steamers of a large class now pass through the locks into Lake Superior,

[*] Settled in 1668, by the French.

greatly facilitating trade and commerce. The village on the American side is pleasantly situated near the foot of the rapids, and contains a court-house and jail; a Presbyterian, a Methodist, and a Roman Catholic church; 2 hotels, and 15 or 20 stores and storehouses, besides a few manufacturing establishments, and about 1,200 inhabitants. Many of the inhabitants and Indians in the vicinity are engaged in the fur trade and fisheries, the latter being an important and profitable occupation. Summer visitors flock to this place and the Lake Superior country for health and pleasure. The *Chippewa House*, a well kept hotel on the American side, and one on the Canadian side of the river, both afford good accommodations.

FORT BRADY is an old and important United States military post contiguous to this frontier village, where are barracks for a full garrison of troops. It commands the St. Mary's River and the approach to the mouth of the canal.

SAUT STE. MARIE, C. W., is a scattered settlement, where is located a part of the Hudson Bay Company. Here is a steamboat landing, a hotel, and two or three stores, including the Hudson Bay Company's; and it has from 500 to 600 inhabitants. Indians of the Chippewa tribe reside in the vicinity in considerable numbers, they having the exclusive right to take fish in the waters contiguous to the rapids. They also employ themselves in running the rapids in their frail canoes, when desired by citizens or strangers—this being one of the most exhilarating enjoyments for those fond of aquatic sports. (*See Engraving.*)

SAULT ST. MARIE—FROM AMERICAN SIDE.

PORTAGE ROUTE FROM LAKE SUPERIOR TO LAKE WINNIPEG.

STARTING FROM FORT WILLIAM, C. W.

KAMINISTAQUOIAH RIVER, emptying into Thunder Bay of Lake Superior, forms the west boundary of Canada proper; to the north and west lies the extensive region or country known as the *Hudson Bay Company's Territory.* Here commences the great *Portage Road* to Rainy Lake, Lake of the Woods, and the Red River settlement; also, to Lake Winnipeg, Norway House, and York Factory, situated on Hudson Bay. At the mouth of the Kaministaquoiah stands *Fort William.* "The banks of the river average in height from eight to twenty feet; the soil is alluvial and very rich. The vegetation all along its banks is remarkably thrifty and luxuriant in its appearance. The land is well timbered; there are found in great abundance, the fir-tree, birch, tamarack, poplar, elm, and the spruce, There is also white pine, but not in great plenty. Wild hops and peas are found in abundance, and some bushes and other flowering shrubs; in many places cover the banks down to the very margin of the river, adorning them with beauty, and often filling the air with fragrance. The land on this river up to the Mountain Portage (32 miles), and for a long way back, is unsurpassed in richness and beauty by any lands in British America."

The *Mountain Fall,* situated on this stream, is thus described: "We had great difficulty in finding it at first, but, guided by its thundering roar, through such a thicket of brush, thorns and briars, as I never before thought of, we reached the spot from whence it was visible. The whole river plunged in one broad white sheet, through a space not more than fifty feet wide, and over a precipice higher, by many feet, than the *Niagara* Falls. The concave sheet comes together about three-fourths of the way to the bottom, from whence the spray springs high into the air, bedewing and whitening the precipitous and wild looking crags with which the fall is composed, and clothing with drapery of foam the gloomy pines, that hang about the clefts and fissures of the rocks. The falls and the whole surrounding scenery, for sublimity, wildness, and novel grandeur, exceeds any thing of the kind I ever saw."—*Rev. J. Ryerson's Tour.*

The danger of navigating these mountain streams, in a birch canoe, is greater than many would expect who had never witnessed the force of the current sometimes encountered. Mr. Ryerson remarks: "During the day we passed a large number of strong and some dangerous rapids. Several times the canoe, in spite of the most strenuous exertions of the men, was driven back. such was the violence of the currents. On one occasion such was the force of the stream, that though four strong men were holding the rope, it was wrenched out of their hands in an instant, and we were hurled down the rapids with violent speed, at the mercy of the foaming waves and irresistible torrent, until fortunately in safety we reached an eddy below." (*See Engraving.*)

DOG LAKE is an expansion of the river, distant by its winding course, 76 miles from its mouth. Other lakes and expansions of streams are passed on the route westward.

"The SAVAN, or PRAIRIE PORTAGE, 120 miles from Fort William, by portage route, forms the height of land between Lake Superior and the waters falling into Lake Winnipeg; it is between three and four miles long, and a continuous cedar swamp from one end to the other, and is therefore very properly named the *Savan* or *Swamp*

Portage. It lies seven or eight hundred feet above Lakes Superior and Winnipeg, and 1,483 feet above the sea."

The SAVAN RIVER, which is first formed by the waters of the Swamp, enters into the *Lac Du Mille*, or the Lake of Thousands, so called because of the innumerable islands which are in it. This lake is comparatively narrow, being sixty or seventy miles in length.

The *River Du Mille*, the outlet of the Lake, is a precipitous stream, whereon are several portages, before entering into Lac La Pluie, distant 350 miles from Fort William.

RAINY LAKE, or *Lac la Pluie*, through which runs the boundary between the United States and Canada, is a most beautiful sheet of water; it is forty-eight miles long, and averages about ten miles in breadth. It receives the waters flowing westward from the dividing ridge separating the waters flowing into Lake Superior.

RAINY LAKE RIVER, the outlet of the lake of the same name, is a magnificent stream of water; it has a rapid current and averages about a quarter of a mile in width; its banks are covered with the richest foliage of every hue; the trees in the vicinity are large and varied, consisting of ash, cedar, poplar, oak, birch, and red and white pines; also an abundance of flowers of gaudy and variegated colors. The climate is also very fine, with a rich soil, and well calculated to sustain a dense population as any part of Canada.

The LAKE OF THE WOODS, or *Lac Du Bois*, 68 miles in length, and from fifteen to twenty-five miles wide, is a splendid sheet of water, dotted all over with hundreds of beautiful islands, many of which are covered with a heavy and luxuriant foliage. Warm and frequent showers occur here in May and June bringing forth vegetation at a rapid rate, although situated on the 49th degree of north latitude, from whence extends *westward* to the Pacific

PULLING A CANOE UP THE RAPIDS.

Ocean, the boundary line between the United States and Canada.

"There is nothing, I think, better calculated to awaken the more solemn feelings of our nature, than these noble lakes studded with innumerable islets, suddenly bursting on the traveller's view as he emerges from the sombre forest rivers of the American wilderness. The clear, unruffled water, stretching out on the horizon; here intersecting the heavy and luxuriant foliage of an hundred woody isles, or reflecting the wood-clad mountains on its margin, clothed in all the variegated hues of autumn; and there glittering with dazzling brilliancy in the bright rays of the evening sun, or rippling among the reeds and rushes of some shallow bay, where hundreds of wild fowl chatter as they feed with varied cry, rendering more apparent, rather than disturbing the solemn stillness of the scene: all tend to raise the soul from nature up to nature's God, and remind one of the beautiful passage of Scripture, 'O Lord, how marvellous are thy works, in wisdom hast thou made them all; the earth is full of thy riches.'" —*Ballantyne.*

The WINNIPEG RIVER, the outlet of the Lake of the Woods, is a rapid stream, of large size, falling into Winnipeg Lake, 3 miles below *Fort Alexander,* one of the Hudson Bay Company's Posts. A great number of Indians resort to the Fort every year, besides a number of families who are residents in the vicinity, here being one of their favorite haunts.

Rev. Mr. Ryerson remarks:—"The scenery for many miles around is strikingly beautiful. The climate for Hudson's Bay Territory is here remarkably fine and salubrious, the land amazingly rich and productive. The water in Lakes Lac La Pluie, Lac Du Bois, Winnipeg, &c., is not deep, and because of their wide surface and great shallowness, during the summer season, they become exceedingly warm; this has a wonderful effect on the temperature of the atmosphere in the adjacent neighborhoods, and no doubt makes the great difference in the climate (or at least is one of the principal causes of it), in these parts, to the climate and vegetable productions in the neighborhood of Lake Superior, near Fort William. They grow spring wheat here to perfection, and vegetation is rapid, luxuriant, and comes to maturity before frosts occur."

The whole region of country surrounding Lake Winnipeg, the Red River country, as well as the Assiniboine and Saskatchewan country, are all sooner or later destined to sustain a vigorous and dense population.

LAKE WINNIPEG,

Situated between 50° and 55° north latitude, is about 300 miles long, and in several parts more than 50 miles broad; having an estimated area of 8,500 square miles.* Lake Winnipeg receives the waters of numerous rivers, which, in the aggregate, drain an area of about 400,000 square miles. The *Saskatchewan* (the river that runs fast) is its most important tributary. The Assiniboine, the Red River of the North, and Winnipeg River are its other largest tributaries, altogether discharging an immense amount of water into this great inland lake. It is elevated about 700 feet above Hudson Bay, and discharges its surplus waters through *Nelson River,* a large and magnificent stream, which like the St. Lawrence is filled with islands and numerous rapids,

---

* LAKE BAIKAL, the most extensive body of fresh water on the Eastern Continent, situated in Southern Siberia, between lat. 51° and 55° north, is about 370 miles in length, 45 miles average width, and about 900 miles in circuit; being somewhat larger than Lake Winnipeg in area. Its depth in some places is very great, being in part surrounded by high mountains. The *Yenisei*, its outlet, flows north into the Arctic Ocean.

preventing navigation entirely below Cross Lake.

Lakes *Manitobah* and *Winnipego-sis*, united, are nearly of the same length as Winnipeg, lying 40 or 50 miles westward. Nearly the whole country between Lake Winnipeg and its western rivals is occupied by smaller lakes, so that between the valley of the Assiniboine and the eastern shore of Winnipeg fully one-third is under water. These lakes, both large and small, are shallow, and in the same water area show much uniformity in depth and coast line.

Lakes in the Valley of the Saskatchewan.

	Length in miles.	Breadth in miles.	Elevation in feet.	Area in m's.
Winnipeg,	280	57	628	8,500
Manitobah,	122	24	670	2,000
Winnipego-sis,	120	27	692	2,000
St. Martin,	30	16	655	350
Cedar,	30	25	688	350
Dauphin,	21	12	700	200

All the smaller lakes lie west of Lake Winnipeg, which receives their surplus waters; the whole volume, with the large streams, flowing into *Nelson River*, discharges into Hudson Bay, near York Factory, in 57° north latitude. The navigation of the latter stream is interrupted by falls and rapids, having a descent of 628 feet in its course of about 350 miles.

"The climate in the region of the above lakes and the Red River Settlement will compare not unfavorably with that of Kingston and Toronto, Canada West. The Spring generally opens somewhat earlier, but owing to the proximity of Lake Winnipeg which is late of breaking up, the weather is always variable until the middle of May. The slightest breeze from the north or northwest, blowing over the frozen surface of that inland sea, has an immediate effect on the temperature during the Spring months. On the other hand, the Fall is generally open, with mild, dry, and pleasant weather."

Red River of the North.

This interesting section of country being closely connected with the Upper Lakes, and attracting much attention at the present time, we subjoin the following extract from "MINNESOTA AND DACOTA," by C. C. Andrews:

"It is common to say that settlements have not been extended beyond Crow Wing, Minnesota. This is only technically true. A few facts in regard to the people who live four or five hundred miles to the north will best illustrate the nature of the climate and its adaptedness to agriculture.

"There is a settlement at *Pembina*, near the 49th parallel of latitude, where the dividing line between British America and the United States crosses the Red River of the North. Pembina is said to have about 600 inhabitants. It is situated on the Pembina River. It is an Indian-French word meaning '*Cranberry*.' Men live there who were born there, and it is in fact an old settlement. It was founded by British subjects, who thought they had located on British soil. The greater part of its inhabitants are half-breeds, who earn a comfortable livelihood in fur-hunting and farming. It is 460 miles northwest of St. Paul, and 330 miles distant from Crow Wing. Notwithstanding the distance, there is considerable communication between the two places. West of Pembina, about thirty miles, is a settlement called *St. Joseph*, situated near a large mythological body of water called *Miniwakin*, or Devil's Lake.

"Now let me say something about this RED RIVER of the North, for it is beginning to be a great feature in this upper country. It runs north and empties into Lake Winnipeg, which connects with Hudson Bay by Nelson River. It is a muddy and sluggish stream, navigable to the mouth of the Sioux Wood River for vessels of three feet draught for four months in the year, so that the extent of its navigation within Minnesota alone (between Pembina and the mouth of Sioux Wood River) is 400 miles. Buffaloes still feed on its western banks. Its tributaries are numerous and copious, abounding with the choicest kind of game, and skirted with a various and beautiful foliage. It cannot be many years before this magnificent valley (together with the Saskatchewan) shall pour its products into our markets, and be the theatre of a busy and genial life.

"*Red River Settlement* is seventy miles north of Pembina, and lies on both sides of the river. Its population is estimated at 10,000 souls. It owes its origin and growth to the enterprise and success of the Hudson Bay Company. Many of the settlers came from Scotland, but the most were from Canada. They speak English and Canadian French. The English style of society is well kept up, whether we regard the Church with its bishop, the trader with his wine-cellar, the scholar with his library, the officer with his sinecure, or their paper currency. The great business of the settlement, of course, is the fur traffic.

"An immense amount of Buffalo skins is taken in summer and autumn, while in the winter smaller but more valuable furs are procured. The Indians also enlist in the hunts; and it is estimated that upward of $200,000 worth of furs are annually taken from our territory and sold to the Hudson Bay Company. It is high time indeed that a military post should be established somewhere on Red River by our government.

"The Hudson Bay Company is now a powerful monopoly. Not so magnificent and potent as the East India Company, it is still a powerful combination, showering opulence on its members, and reflecting a peculiar feature in the strength and grandeur of the British empire—a power which, to use the eloquent language of Daniel Webster, 'has dotted over the whole surface of the globe with her possessions and military posts, whose morning drum-beat following the sun, and keeping company with the hours, circles the earth daily with one continuous and unbroken strain of martial music.' The company is growing richer every year, and its jurisdiction and its lands will soon find an availability never dreamed of by its founders, unless, as may possibly happen, *popular sovereignty steps in to grasp the fruits* of its long apprenticeship."

The Charter of the Hudson Bay Company expired, by its own limitation, in 1860, and the question of annexing this vast domain to Canada, or forming a separate province, is now deeply agitating the British public, both in Canada and in the mother country.

TABLE OF DISTANCES,

From Fort William, SITUATED AT THE MOUTH OF THE KAMISTAQUOIAH RIVER, **to Fort Alexander**, AT THE HEAD OF LAKE WINNIPEG.

	Miles.	
Fort William..	0	
Parapluie Portage..	25	
(8 Portages)		
Dog Portage...	51	76
(5 Portages)		
Savan or Swamp Portage*..................................	54	130
Thousand Islands Lake......................................	57	187
(2 Portages)		
Sturgeon Lake...	71	258
(4 Portages)		
Lac La Croix...	25	283
(5 Portages)		
Rainy Lake...	40	323
Rainy Lake River...	38	361
Lake of the Woods...	83	444
Rat Portage..	68	512
Fort Alexander..	125	637

From Fort Alexander to Fort Garry
OR RED RIVER SETTLEMENT, BY WATER.

	Miles.	
To Pointe de Grand Marais.................................		24
" Red River Beacon...	25	49
" Lower Fort..	23	72
" Fort Garry...	24	96

From Fort Alexander to Norway House, passing through Lake Winnipeg, 300 miles.

From Norway House to York Factory, passing through Oxford Lake and Hayes River, 400 miles.

* Summit, elevated 840 feet above Lake Superior.

HOTELS.

TREMONT HOUSE,

CHICAGO, ILL.,
Situated on corner of Lake and Dearborn Streets.

Re-built, re-modeled, and re-furnished, in 1862, at a cost of $160,000. It contains all the modern improvements, and is one of the best-appointed Hotels in the country. It has

NUMEROUS SUITES OF ROOMS,

with Baths, Water, etc., attached, for the accommodation of families.

It is easy of access to all the different Railroad Dépôts, Places of Amusement, and Steamboat Landings.

GAGE & DRAKE, Proprietors.

HOTELS.

SHERMAN HOUSE,

CHICAGO, ILLINOIS.

This HOTEL is centrally located on the corner of Clark and Randolph Streets, pposite Court House Square; was built, in 1860, of Athens Marble, and has all the modern improvements, including a Passenger Elevator to convey the guests to and from the several stories of the house. In fact, it is in every particular, as

COMPLETE AND MAGNIFICENT AN ESTABLISHMENT

as there is in the United States.

DAVID A. GAGE, } Proprietors.
CHARLES C. WAITE,

ILLINOIS CENTRAL R. R

CHICAGO AND CAIRO.

The only Direct Route to **CAIRO, MEMPHIS, VICKSBURG, NEW ORLEANS, MOBILE,** and all Points **SOUTH.**

It also forms with its Connections a direct and expeditious route to **PEORIA, SPRINGFIELD, ALTON, ST. LOUIS, KANSAS CITY,** and all parts of the **SOUTH-WEST.**

TWO DAILY EXPRESS TRAINS

leave CHICAGO from the Great Central Depot, foot of Lake and South Water Streets.

AT GILMAN,

81 miles from Chicago, connections are made with Toledo, Peoria, and Warsaw Railroad, east for Logansport—west for Peoria. Connecting at

TOLONE,

137 miles from Chicago, with Toledo, Wabash, and Western R. R., east for Danville and Lafayette—west for Decatur, Springfield, Jacksonville, Quincy, and Keokuk. Connecting at

MATTOON,

172 miles from Chicago, with St. Louis, Alton, and Terre Haute R. R., east for Terre Haute, Indianapolis, and Cincinnati—west for Alton, St. Louis, Kansas City, Leavenworth, Lawrence, and Topeka. At

ODIN,

244 miles from Chicago, with Ohio and Mississippi R. R., east for Vincennes, Evansville, Louisville, and Cincinnati—west for St. Louis, Kansas City, Leavenworth, Lawrence, and Topeka. At

CAIRO,

365 miles from Chicago, connections are made with Mobile and Ohio R. R., for Jackson, Tenn., Memphis, Grand Junction, Holly Springs, Oxford, Canton, Grenada, Columbus, Meridian, Jackson, Miss., Vicksburg, Selma, Mobile, and New Orleans.

Connections are also made at CAIRO with Steamboats for all points on the Lower Mississippi.

ELEGANT SLEEPING CARS

on all Night Trains. Saloon Cars with raised roofs and **RUTLAND PATENT DUSTERS AND VENTILATORS.** Also, SMOKING CARS on Day Trains.

☞ **Through Tickets and Baggage Checks** issued to all important points.

M. HUGHITT, General Supt. Chicago.
W. P. JOHNSON, General Passenger Agent.

ILLINOIS CENTRAL RAILROAD.

DUNLEITH AND CAIRO.

The only Direct Route to **St. Louis, Cairo, Memphis, Vicksburg, New Orleans, Mobile**, and all parts of the **South** and **South-west**.

It is also the Direct Route from the West and North-west to Chicago and all Eastern Cities.

TWO DAILY EXPRESS TRAINS leave Dunleith (opposite Dubuque) morning and evening, on arrival of Steamers from St. Paul and Trains from the West.

Connecting at **Freeport**, 67 miles from Dunleith, with the Galena Divisions of Chicago and North-western R. R., for Rockford, Belvidere, Elgin, and Chicago. Also connecting at this point with the Western Union R. R., for Beloit, Racine, Sarana, and Milwaukee.

At **Dixon**, 103 miles from Dunleith, connections are made with the Iowa Division of Chicago and North western R. R., east for Chicago—west for Fulton, Clinton, Lyons, Cedar Rapids, and Des Moines.

At **Mendota**, 131 miles from Dunleith, connections are made with the Chicago, Burlington, and Quincy R. R., east for Chicago, west for Galesburg, Burlington, Quincy, Keokuk, and St. Joseph.

At **La Salle**, 147 miles from Dunleith, connections are made with the Chicago and Rock Island R. R., east for Joliet and Chicago, west for Peoria, Rock Island, Muscatine, Iowa City, and Des Moines.

At **El Paso**, 189 miles from Dunleith, connections are made with Toledo, Peoria, and Warsaw R. R., east for Logansport, west for Peoria.

At **Bloomington**, 207 miles from Dunleith, connections are made with Chicago and Alton R. R., for Springfield, Alton, and St. Louis.

At **Decatur**, 251 miles from Dunleith, connections are made with Toledo, Wabash, and Western R. R., east for Lafayette, Logansport, Fort Wayne, and Toledo, west for Springfield, Jacksonville, Quincy, and Keokuk.

At **Pana**, 283 miles from Dunleith, connections are made with St. Louis, Alton, and Terre Haute R. R., east for Terre Haute, Indianapolis, Louisville, Cincinnati, Wheeling, Pittsburgh, Baltimore, &c., west for Alton, St. Louis, Kansas City, Leavenworth, Lawrence, Topeka, &c.

At **Sandoval**, 337 miles from Dunleith, connections are made with Ohio and Mississippi R. R., east for Vincennes, Evansville, Louisville, and Cincinnati, west for St. Louis, Kansas City, Leavenworth, Lawrence, Topeka, &c.

At **Cairo**, 456 miles from Dunleith, connections are made with Mobile and Ohio R. R., going south for Jackson, Tenn., Memphis, Grand Junction, Holly Springs, Oxford, Grenada, Columbus, Canton, Meridian, Jackson, Miss., Vicksburg, Selma, Mobile, and New Orleans; connections are also made at Cairo with Steamboats for all points on the Lower Mississippi.

Elegant Sleeping Cars attached to Night Trains.

Through Tickets and Baggage Checks issued to all important points.

Passengers, to avail themselves of quick time, combined with comfort and safety, should see that their Tickets are via Illinois Central R. R.

W. P. JOHNSON,	**M. HUGHITT,**
Gen'l Passenger Agt., Chicago.	*Gen'l Supt., Chicago.*

The Direct Route to Central Illinois,
MISSOURI, KANSAS, NEBRASKA,
Colorado, Idaho, Utah, Nevada & California.

CHICAGO,
BURLINGTON & QUINCY,
AND
HANNIBAL & ST. JOSEPH
RAILROADS.

TWO TRAINS DAILY LEAVE CHICAGO

ON ARRIVAL OF TRAINS FROM THE EAST, MAKING DIRECT CONNECTIONS FOR

QUINCY, HANNIBAL,
ST. JOSEPH,
ATCHISON, LEAVENWORTH, KANSAS CITY,
Lawrence, Topeka, Nebraska City, Omaha City & Council Bluffs.

HALLIDAY'S OVERLAND MAIL & EXPRESS CO.'S LINE OF STAGES
Leave Atchison daily, for Denver, Central City, Bannock, Salt Lake, Virginia City, Austin, and all principal States and Territories west of the MISSOURI RIVER.

STEAM PACKETS ON THE MISSOURI RIVER
In Direct Connection with HANNIBAL AND ST. JOSEPH RAILROAD from St. Joseph, for Nebraska City, Omaha City, Council Bluffs, &c.

☞ The CHICAGO, BURLINGTON & QUINCY RAILROAD is thoroughly equipped with 12-wheel Coaches, with RUTTAN'S PATENT VENTILATORS AND DUSTERS, entirely avoiding the Heat and Dust of Summer. ☞ The SLEEPING CARS on this Road are of the MOST IMPROVED PATTERN, and fitted up in Magnificent Style; equal, if not superior, to any on this continent.

Baggage Checked Through from all parts of the East to the Missouri River! Tickets for Sale at the Principal Ticket Offices throughout the Country.

SAMUEL POWELL,   **ROBERT HARRIS,**
General Ticket Agent, Chicago.   *General Superintendent, Chicago.*

THE PENNSYLVANIA CENTRAL
DOUBLE-TRACK RAILROAD.

SHORTEST, QUICKEST, AND BEST ROUTE
BETWEEN THE EAST AND WEST.

On the arrival of Passenger Trains from the West, at the Union Depot, PITTSBURGH, **Through Trains** leave as follows:

DAY EXPRESS, 2.30 A. M. (Except Sunday).
CINCINNATI EXPRESS, 9.00 A. M. (Except Sunday).
FAST MAIL, 11.50 P. M. (Except Sunday).
PHILADELPHIA EXPRESS, 4.05 P. M. Every Day.
FAST LINE, 10.10 P. M. (Except Sunday).

Running through without change of Cars to **Harrisburg, Philadelphia, Baltimore,** and **New York** (via Allentown), HOURS IN ADVANCE OF OTHER LINES, connecting direct for all New England Towns and Washington City.

This is the only route by which passengers leaving St. Louis, Cairo, and Quincy Saturday morning, Chicago, Jeffersonville, and Indianapolis Saturday evening, RUN THROUGH DIRECT to Eastern Cities, arriving

24 HOURS IN ADVANCE OF OTHER ROUTES!
ELEGANT STATE-ROOM SLEEPING CARS
ARE ATTACHED TO ALL NIGHT TRAINS.

Baggage Checked Through and Transferred Free!
☞ Fare always as low as by other routes.

H. W. GWINNER, Gen. Ticket Agent, Philadelphia.
T. L. KIMBALL, Ass't G. W. P. Agent, Chicago, Ill.

Office, Metropolitan Block, Chicago.

FREIGHTS.

By this Route, Freight of all descriptions can be forwarded to and from Philadelphia, New York, Boston, or Baltimore, BY RAILROAD DIRECT, to and from any point on Western Railways, and in connection with Steamers, to all accessible points on the Lakes and Rivers of the North-west, West, and South-west.

LIVE STOCK by this route are provided with superior Yard accommodations, especially at Harrisburg, where a choice is offered of the **Philadelphia, New York,** and **Baltimore Markets.**

This will also be found the shortest, quickest, and most direct route for Stock to New York (via Allentown), and with fewest changes.

☞ The RATES OF FREIGHT to and from points in the West by the Pennsylvania Central Railroad are as *favorable as* are charged *by other Railroad Companies.*

CHICAGO
AND
NORTHWESTERN RAILWAY.

Connections are made with Splendid Packets at DUNLEITH, PRAIRIE DU CHIEN, and LA CROSSE, for points on the

UPPER MISSISSIPPI RIVER.

First Class Tickets include Meals and State Rooms on the Steamers.

☛Connections are made at Green Bay, with fine steamers for Escanaba on Little Bay de Noc, thence by the Peninsular Railroad to Marquette, and the Iron and Copper Mines. For LAKE SUPERIOR this is the shortest and most direct route. The Iowa Division of this Company is completed to Boonsboro', 343 miles west of Chicago. Trains running through without change of Cars at the Mississippi River; and 25 miles less Staging to Des Moines, Council Bluffs, and Omaha than any other route. Superior arranged

SLEEPING CARS,

on Night Trains, are run to Cedar Rapids, Dunleith, Prairie du Chien, Fond du Lac, and Green Bay.

☞ Passengers for any point West or Northwest of Chicago, to avail themselves of the many advantages offered by this Company, should be particular and ask for Tickets *via* "CHICAGO & NORTHWESTERN RAILWAY."

B. F. PATRICK, Gen'l Passenger Agent, Chicago.

GEORGE L. DUNLAP, Gen'l Superintendent.

CHICAGO
AND
NORTHWESTERN RAILWAY,

GRAND CONSOLIDATED LINE.
Comprising all principal Railroads from Chicago directly
WEST & NORTHWEST.

Chicago and Northwestern Railway.....Wisconsin Division, Chicago to Green Bay.
Galena and Chicago Union Railway......Galena   do.   Chicago to Freeport.
Dixon Air-Line Railroad..................Galena   do.   Chicago to Fulton.
Cedar Rapids and Missouri River Line...Iowa   do.   Fulton to Nevada, Iowa.
Kenosha, Rockford, and Rock Island Railroad.................Kenosha to Rockford.
     Fox River Valley Railroad and Beloit and Madison Branch.

SIX EXPRESS TRAINS LEAVE CHICAGO DAILY
On the different branches of the
Chicago & Northwestern Railway,

In Connection with Trains from the East and South, for Dixon, Fulton, Clinton, Cedar Rapids, Nevada, Des Moines, Council Bluffs, and Omaha; Rockford, Beloit, Freeport, Mineral Point, Galena, Dunleith, Dubuque, Independence, and Cedar Falls; Janesville, Madison, Prairie du Chien, La Crosse, St. Paul, Watertown, Fond du Lac, Oshkosh, Ripon, Berlin, Green Bay, Escanaba, Marquette, and all points in

Northern Illinois, Iowa, Wisconsin, Minnesota,
and the
LAKE SUPERIOR COUNTRY.

Direct Railway Route from Lake Michigan to the Mississippi River.

Western Union Railway,

(Formerly Racine and Mississippi and Northern Illinois Railroad.)

STATIONS.	MILES.	STATIONS,	MILES.
RACINE	0	Mt. CARROLL	28-131
ELKHORN	40	SAVANNA	11-142
CLINTON	18-58	FULTON	17-159
BELOIT	10-68	ALBANY	6-165
FREEPORT	35-103	PORT BYRON	15-180

This road connects at FULTON, on the Mississippi, with the IOWA DIVISION of the Chicago and North-western Railway, and at Port Byron, Ill., with the Chicago and Rock Island Railroad, and Railroads running through Central Iowa.

THE RACINE & MISSISSIPPI AND NORTHERN ILLINOIS RAILWAYS, recently consolidated under the name of the **WESTERN UNION RAILROAD CO.**, and operated under one management, make a continuous route from Racine, on Lake Michigan, to Savanna, Fulton, and Port Byron, on the Mississippi river.

The route, in connection with the Milwaukee & Chicago Railway, is the shortest line from Milwaukee to the Mississippi river; distance, 165 miles. The railway passes through the most beautiful section of the States of Wisconsin and Illinois—the lands on the route being unsurpassed for farming purposes.

This line is also directly connected with the Chicago & North-western Railway, making a through route from Chicago; also from Janesville, Madison, Oshkosh, Fond du Lac, Appleton, and Green Bay—rendering it a delightful route for the traveler.

At FREEPORT, the line connects with the Illinois Central Railway, making a through route to Warren, Galena, Dunleith, Dubuque, &c.

At SAVANNA, the St. Louis and St. Paul Packets call regularly, and the Northern Line of Steamboats (running daily each way between Dubuque and Rock Island) make close connections with the passenger trains on the Line. Savanna and Sabula are connected by a steam ferry—the latter place being on the most direct route to Maquoketa, and points in Central Iowa. The roads from Sabula are preferred by emigrants crossing the Plains.

Passengers from Milwaukee, and all eastern points of Wisconsin, will find this the most direct and cheapest route to go down the Mississippi. Passengers and goods by Lake, landed at Racine, can reach the Mississippi river by this line more expeditiously than by any other route.

☞ THROUGH TICKETS sold by Eastern Roads, and at the Chicago & North-western Depot, at Chicago; and at the Milwaukee & Chicago Depot, Milwaukee, for Beloit, Freeport, Savanna, Dunleith, and intermediate points.   G. A. THOMSON, *President, Racine, Wis.*

R. C. TATE, *Superintendent, Racine, Wis.*

GOODRICH'S LAKE MICHIGAN
STEAMBOAT LINE!

THE STEAMERS

SEA BIRD, Capt. H. McHENRY

COMET, Capt. JOHN MORRIS,

WILL LEAVE ALTERNATELY FOR

Kenosha, Racine, Milwaukee, Pt. Washington,

SHEBOYGAN, MANITOWOC and TWO RIVERS,

EVERY MORNING (Sundays Excepted), at 9 o'clock.

☞ Saturday's Boat leaves in the Evening, and goes through to KEWANEE and AHNAPEE.

Fare to **MILWAUKEE**, Meals Included, only - - $2.00
" " **RACINE**, " " " 1.50
" " **KENOSHA**, " " " 1.25

☞ Shippers can rely on prompt dispatch of all goods delivered up to 8 o'clock A. M.

FOR GRAND HAVEN AND MUSKEGAN

The Large and Splendid Low-Pressure Side-Wheel Steamer

PLANET!

Capt. BEN WILKINS,

Will leave CHICAGO for GRAND HAVEN and MUSKEGAN every

Monday, Wednesday, and Friday Evenings, at 7 o'clock.

Returning, will leave MUSKEGAN and GRAND HAVEN every

Tuesday, Thursday, and Saturday Evenings.

☞ The PLANET is the largest, finest, and only Low-Pressure Side-Wheel Steamer on this Route, and has unequaled accommodations for passengers.

For Further Information, Freight, or Passage, apply to

A. E. GOODRICH,

Office and Docks BELOW Rush St. Bridge,

CHICAGO.

NORTH-WESTERN UNION PACKET COMPANY.

STEAMERS of this Company run from DUBUQUE and PRAIRIE DU CHIEN to ST. PAUL, forming a DAILY LINE.

DISTANCE, 360 Miles; USUAL TIME, 2 days; FARE, $10,00.

The following first class STEAMERS compose this Line:

MILWAUKEE	Capt. E. V. HOLCOMBE.
ITASKA	Capt. N. F. WEBB.
PHIL. SHERIDAN	Capt. J. T. WEST.
KEY CITY	Capt. W. H. LAWTON.
JENNIE BALDWIN	Capt. W. H. GABBERT.

Blanchard & Wellington, Agents,
DUBUQUE, IOWA.

J. H. HOUSTON, Agent,
PRAIRIE DU CHIEN, WIS.

STEAMERS running from LA CROSSE to ST. PAUL, forming a Daily Line.

Distance, 206 Miles; Fare, $6 00.

WAR EAGLE	Capt. A. MITCHELL.
CITY OF ST. PAUL	Capt. L. W. MOULTON.

M. B. COON, Agent,
LA CROSSE, WIS.

CHARLES THOMPSON, Agent,
ST. PAUL, MINN.

NORTH-WESTERN UNION PACKET COMPANY.

NEW TIME TABLE.

Two Daily Passenger Steamers
WILL LEAVE
SAINT PAUL.

THE
MORNING BOAT

Will leave at 8 o'clock for
LA CROSSE, PRAIRIE DU CHIEN & DUNLIETH,
CONNECTING

At LA CROSSE with the MORNING EX-
PRESS TRAIN, at 6 o'clock,
At PRAIRIE DU CHIEN at 5 P. M.,
AND
At DUNLIETH at 5 A. M.

THE
EVENING BOAT

Will leave at 9 P. M.
For LA CROSSE,
And connect with the next afternoon train at 5 o'clock.

THE ABOVE BOATS WILL RUN
Exclusively for Passengers,
AND WILL MAKE
SURE CONNECTIONS
WITH THE ABOVE TRAINS.

CHARLES THOMPSON,
TICKET AGENT.

OFFICE—Corner of Levee and Jackson Streets, St. Paul.

LAKE SUPERIOR STEAMBOAT ROUTE.

LAKE SUPERIOR LINE

FROM

CLEVELAND and DETROIT.

1866.  **1866.**

The magnificent Steamers mentioned below will leave CLEVELAND and DETROIT, forming a Daily Line to all *Lake Superior Ports;* connecting at Marquette, Mich., with the Railway Line to Chicago, Ill., and to St. Paul, Minn.

KEWEENAW,	**IRON CITY,**
Captain A. STEWART.	Captain JOHN HALLORAN.
NORTHERN LIGHT,	**LAC-LA-BELLE,**
Captain M. H. MURCH.	Captain JOHN SPAULDING.
S. D. CALDWELL,	**METEOR,**
Captain J. M. LEWIS.	Captain T. WILSON.
IRONSIDES,	**ILLINOIS,**
Captain J. E. TURNER.	Captain B. G. SWEET.
DUBUQUE,	**CONCORD,**
Captain McLEAN.	Captain A. McINTYRE.
MINERAL ROCK,	**GOV. CUSHMAN,**
Captain JOHN McKAY.	Captain H. W. THOMPSON.

☞ Steamers of this Line touch at Port Huron, or Sarnia, Can., on the evening of the day they leave Detroit.

The round trip of more than 2,000 miles, passing through Lakes Erie, St. Clair, Huron, and Superior, and the beautiful Rivers Detroit, St. Clair, and the Ste. Marie, with its numerous Islands, presenting to the Tourist for Health or Pleasure, more varied attractions than any other on the continent of America.

CLEVELAND AGENTS:	DETROIT AGENTS:
PETTIT & HOLLAND.	S. P. BRADY & CO.
R. HANNA & CO.	BUCKLEY & CO.
H. GARRETSON & CO.	JOHN HUTCHINGS.

MINNESOTA
CENTRAL RAILWAY,

1866.  1866.

SUMMER
RUNNING ARRANGEMENT.
Two Daily Trains Each Way.

TRAINS WILL RUN AS FOLLOWS.

LEAVES.		ARRIVES.
8.45 A. M., 3.40 P. M.,	MINNEAPOLIS.	10.40 A. M. 5.45 P. M.
6.00 A. M., 1.40 P. M.,	FARIBAULT.	1.00 P. M. 8.45 P. M.

Trains going North will not stop at FORT SNELLING.

The Morning Train going South, and the Evening Train going North will not stop at Westcott or Castle Rock. All other trains will stop at Minnehaha, Fort Snelling, Westcott, and Castle Rock on signal.

Passengers leaving Faribault at 6 A. M., and Minneapolis at 8.45 A. M., connect with the 10.30 A. M. Boat from St. Paul. Passengers from Faribault at 1.40 P. M., and Minneapolis at 3.40 P. M., connect with the 6 P. M. Boat from St. Paul. Fare from Minneapolis to St. Paul as low as by any other route, and omnibus ride at Minneapolis saved. Tickets for sale at the Railway Company's Depot in Minneapolis, and at the Ticket Office of the North-western Union Packet Company, on the Levee, St. Paul.

Persons desiring to visit the interior of the State on their return East can leave Minneapolis or St. Paul in the morning, and arrive at Winona at noon next day, or can leave St. Paul or Minneapolis in the afternoon, and arrive at Winona on the evening of next day, connecting with Boat for La Crosse and points East. This line passes through the heart of the grain growing district of Minnesota, and is made up of one hundred and twenty miles of railway, divided by only forty miles of stage route over splended natural roads. A first class line of four-horse coaches is run daily by the Minnesota Stage Company between the railroad termini at Kasson and Faribault. Fare from St. Paul or Minneapolis to La Crosse, $11.75. Tickets for sale at the Depot of the Railway Company in Minneapolis, and of the Minnesota Stage Company in St. Paul.

D. C. SHEPARD,
General Superintendent, Minneapolis.

FIRST DIVISION
ST. PAUL & PACIFIC
RAILROAD.

Finished from ST. PAUL to BIG LAKE,
50 MILES.

PASSENGER TRAINS RUN AS FOLLOWS:

GOING WEST.

Leaves **St Paul**	8 00 A. M.	3 30 P. M.
" St. Anthony	8 45 "	4 20 "
" Manomin	9 10 "	4 45 "
" Anoka	9 45 "	5 25 "
" Itasca	10 05 "	5 45 "
" Elk River	10 30 "	6 10 "
Arrive at **Big Lake**	11 00 "	6 45 "

GOING EAST.

Leave **Big Lake**	7 00 A. M.	3 00 P. M
" Elk River	7 45 "	3 30 "
" Itasca	8 05 "	3 45 "
" Anoka	8 35 "	4 10 "
" Manomin	9 10 "	4 45 "
" St. Anthony	9 45 "	5 15 "
Arrive at **St. Paul**	10 30 "	5 55 "

☞ Purchase tickets at the Stations, before entering the Cars, at a discount from the regular train rate.

Passenger trains meet at Manomin. Persons wishing to make a short pleasure trip can take the 8 A. M. or 3.30 P. M. train from St. Paul, go to Manomin, 18 miles, and return to St. Paul, at 10.30 A. M. or 5.55 P. M., without change of car—gone from St. Paul 2¼ hours, morning or evening.

Passengers must get their baggage checked before it will be carried over the road, and on the arrival of the train at place of destination must present the check and take possession of their baggage, as the Company will not be responsible for the safety of any baggage after its arrival at the Station for which it is checked, it being no part of the business of this Company to receive and store Baggage unless a special contract is made to that effect.

F. R. DELANO, Sup't,

St. Paul, Minn.

www.ingramcontent.com/pod-product-compliance
Lightning Source LLC
Chambersburg PA
CBHW031123160426
43192CB00008B/1089